LOVE DOES

DISCOVER *a* SECRETLY INCREDIBLE LIFE *and* BECOME
LOVE *in a* WORLD FULL *of* DIFFICULT PEOPLE

EVERYBODY ALWAYS

BIBLE STUDY GUIDE | TEN SESSIONS

BOB GOFF

WITH DIXON KINSER

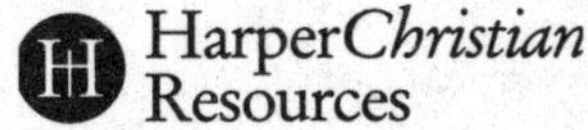

Love Does / Everybody, Always 2-in-1 Bible Study Guide
© 2013, 2018 by Bob Goff

Published in Grand Rapids, Michigan, by HarperChristian Resources. HarperChristian Resources is a registered trademark of HarperCollins Christian Publishing, Inc.

Requests for information should be sent to customercare@harpercollins.com.

ISBN 978-0-310-17479-0 (softcover)
ISBN 978-0-310-17492-9 (ebook)

All Scripture quotations are from the Holy Bible, New International Version®, NIV®. Copyright © 1973, 1978, 1984, 2011 by Biblica, Inc.® Used by permission. All rights reserved worldwide. The "NIV" and "New International Version" are trademarks registered in the United States Patent and Trademark Office by Biblica, Inc.®

Any internet addresses (websites, blogs, etc.) and telephone numbers in this study guide are offered as a resource. They are not intended in any way to be or imply an endorsement by HarperChristian Resources, nor does HarperChristian Resources vouch for the content of these sites and numbers for the life of this study guide.

HarperChristian Resources titles may be purchased in bulk for church, business, fundraising, or ministry use. For information, please e-mail ResourceSpecialist@ChurchSource.com.

First Printing June 2025 / Printed in the United States of America

Contents

How to Use This Guide

Love is practical. It gets out there and does things. It takes risks. It loves even those who are difficult to love. This combined 2-in-1 study, featuring the messages of both *Love Does* and *Everybody, Always*, is designed to give you similar opportunities.

Before you begin, know there are a few ways you can go through this material. You can experience this study with others in a group (such as a Bible study, Sunday school class, or other gathering), or you can go through the content on your own. Either way, the videos are available to view at any time by following the instructions provided with this study guide.

Group Study

Each of the sessions in this study is divided into two parts: (1) a group study section, and (2) a personal study section. The group study section provides a basic framework on how to open your time together, get the most out of the video content, and discuss the key ideas that were presented in the teaching. Each session includes the following:

- **Welcome:** A short opening note about the topic of the session for you to read on your own before you meet as a group.
- **Connect:** A few icebreaker questions to get you and your group members thinking about the topic and interacting with each other.
- **Read:** A short passage from the Bible for you and your group members to review and discuss before the video teaching.
- **Watch:** An outline of the key points covered in each video teaching along with space for you to take notes as you watch each session.
- **Discuss:** Questions to help you and your group reflect on the teaching material presented and apply it to your lives.
- **Respond:** A short personal exercise to help reinforce the key ideas.
- **Pray:** A place for you to record prayer requests and praises for the week.

If you are doing this study in a group, make sure you have your own copy of the study guide so you can write down your thoughts, responses, and reflections in the space provided—and so you have access to the videos via streaming. You will also want to have copies of the *Love Does* and *Everybody, Always* books, as reading these alongside this guide will provide you with deeper insights. (See the notes at the beginning of each group session and personal study section on which chapters of the books you should read before the next group session.)

Finally, keep these points in mind:

- **Facilitation:** If you are doing this study in a group, you will want to appoint someone to serve as a facilitator. This person will be responsible for starting the video and keeping track of time during discussions and activities. If *you* have been chosen for this role, there are some resources in the back of this guide that can help you lead your group through the study.

- **Faithfulness:** Your group is a place where tremendous growth can happen as you reflect on the Bible, ask questions, and learn what God is doing in other people's lives. For this reason, be fully committed to the group and attend each session so you can build trust and rapport with the other members.

- **Friendship:** The goal of any small group is to serve as a place where people can share, learn about God, and build friendships. So seek to make your group a "safe place." Be honest about your thoughts and feelings, but also listen carefully to everyone else's thoughts, feelings, and opinions. Keep anything personal that your group members share in confidence so that you can create a community where people can heal, be challenged, and grow spiritually.

If you are going through this study on your own, read the opening Welcome section and reflect on the questions in the Connect section. Watch the video and use the outline provided to help you take notes. Finally, personalize the questions and exercises in the Discuss and Respond sections. Close by recording any requests you want to pray about during the week.

Personal Study

The personal study is for you to work through on your own during the week. This section includes activities developed around action (called *Do*), Bible study (called *Reflect*), a selected reading from the accompanying books (called *Read*), and ideas for connection with another group member to "compare notes" on what you are learning (called *Interact*). In addition, a *Catch Up* day has been provided if you find that you are behind any week. Go at your own pace, doing a little each day—or tackle the material all at once. Remember to also spend a few moments in silence each day to listen to what God might be saying to you.

Note that if you are doing this study as part of a group, and you are unable to finish (or even start) these personal studies for the week, you should still attend the group time. Be assured that you are still wanted and welcome even if you don't have your "homework" done. The group and personal studies are intended to help you hear from God and apply what he is saying to your life. So . . . as you go through this study, be listening for him to reveal why *Love Does* and what it means for you to love *Everybody, Always*.

Action Guide

Jesus showed us that God's love is *active*. It goes to work. It takes risks. And this is the kind of love that Jesus wants his followers to show to others. But tapping into this type of love takes a different skill set—and it's difficult to know where to start. This is where the Action Guide at the end of this resource comes into play. You will find a number of simple options you can do to serve others in practical ways. Use these ideas as part of your weekly small-group meetings, for special times of service, or even as individual projects to show the people in your world that love is not just an idea . . . but something that actually changes lives.

LOVE DOES

DISCOVER A SECRETLY INCREDIBLE

LIFE IN AN ORDINARY WORLD

A Note from Bob

Welcome to *Love Does*!

All of us have seasons of life when our relationship with God is really humming—those times where our faith and life sync up in all the right ways and everything just seems to work. We also have the other kind of seasons. You know the ones I mean: the seasons where faith and life seem to butt heads. Life gets hard, faith seems stale, and we feel stuck.

If you've ever felt like that, don't go anywhere—this study is for you! This is a study about *God's love* . . . and the most amazing thing about that love is that it's not just a bunch of rules or stuff you have to agree with. God's love is different. It changes things. It brings hope where before there was only despair. It revives faith that feels lifeless. It makes a way forward where there seems to be only a dead end.

It's active. It works. It risks.

God's love . . . *does*.

Tapping into this love requires a different skill set than what it takes to memorize answers for a test or to follow all the traffic laws so you don't get a ticket. This isn't a love you can earn, buy, or win. It's something bigger. Something better. And it just might be something you discover more about by "doing stuff" too.

That's what this study is all about.

Bob Goff

BEFORE GROUP MEETING	Read the introduction and chapters 1–6 in *Love Does* Read the Welcome section (page 6)
GROUP MEETING	Discuss the Connect questions Read the passage for this session and discuss Watch the video teaching for session 1 Discuss the questions that follow as a group Do the closing exercise and pray (pages 7–10)
STUDY 1: *Do*	Complete the personal study (page 12)
STUDY 2: *Reflect*	Complete the personal study (pages 13–14)
STUDY 3: *Read*	Complete the personal study (pages 15–16)
CATCH UP AND READ AHEAD (BEFORE WEEK 2 GROUP MEETING)	Read chapters 7–12 in *Love Does* Complete any unfinished personal studies (page 17)

 | # I'm with You

Love is not just a bunch of stuff
we agree with. Love does.
BOB GOFF

Welcome [READ ON YOUR OWN]

Have you ever had to do something you were afraid to do? Sure. Everyone has. It is a core part of the human experience. Whether it is jumping off a high dive, riding a bike for the first time, or even professing love, each of us at some point has to do something we are scared of—and that's a good thing. Why? Because these experiences teach us important lessons about being human and about our life with God. And what are some of these lessons?

First, when we do things that we are afraid of, we learn that courage is not the same thing as the absence of fear. The first time a child dives into a swimming pool, it is a terrifying experience. No amount of explaining, hand-holding, or encouragement will make the fear go away. To dive into the pool, the child has to act *in spite of* fear. This is the definition of courage. Acting, even when we are afraid, is something we have to do all the time.

Second, after we do something that frightens us the first time, the next time we do it is never as hard. And it is even easier the third time. Although the first jump off the diving board may be terrifying, by the third or fourth time we do it, it may start to be downright fun.

Third, when we try things that seem daunting, our lives actually become more full and vibrant. We might be tempted to think the way to resolve this whole tension of facing our fears is to *avoid risky situations at all costs*. But none of us have that much control over life, and it is actually in these moments that we feel most alive. Have you ever seen a kid go over a skateboard ramp for the first time? Or watched someone complete a rock climb? Often, you'll find them screaming in celebration. Why? Because they just feel so alive! They did it!

So, how does God factor into all of this? And what does any of it have to do with *Love Does*? The *Love Does* experience will encourage you to get out there and "do" things. You will be invited, through the sharing and activities in each session, to engage in some holy risk-taking. Please take this invitation seriously and don't let the opportunity pass you by. Every time you participate in the hands-on portions of this study, you'll be training yourself to see the world as a place where you can act creatively for and with God. You'll become the kind of person who "does" love effortlessly.

For this first session, the question for you to consider is whether you have ever felt stuck trying to integrate your life and your faith. Maybe there was a time when following Jesus was exciting but now things have gotten stale. One of the reasons this often happens is because we stop taking up Jesus' invitation to live a risky, courageous life. We stop doing the things Jesus has called us to do because they seem too scary. So, this week's study in *Love Does* will provide a platform for you to become fully alive, to take risks, and to get involved in bringing heaven to earth. Are you ready? Well, actually, that doesn't matter . . . we're just going to "do" it. So let's jump in with both feet!

Connect [10 MINUTES]

If you or any of your group members don't know each other, take a few minutes to introduce yourselves. Then discuss the following questions:

- If you could describe your expectations for this study in one word, what would that word be?

- Why did you pick the word you did?

Read [10 MINUTES]

Ask someone to read the following passage, and then discuss the questions that follow.

[18] This is how the birth of Jesus the Messiah came about: His mother Mary was pledged to be married to Joseph, but before they came together, she was found to be pregnant through the Holy Spirit. [19] Because Joseph her husband was faithful to the law, and yet did not want to expose her to public disgrace, he had in mind to divorce her quietly.

[20] But after he had considered this, an angel of the Lord appeared to him in a dream and said, "Joseph son of David, do not be afraid to take Mary home as your wife, because what is conceived in her is from the Holy Spirit. [21] She will give birth to a son, and you are to give him the name Jesus, because he will save his people from their sins."

[22] All this took place to fulfill what the Lord had said through the prophet: [23] "The virgin will conceive and give birth to a son, and they will call him Immanuel" (which means "God with us").

MATTHEW 1:18–23

Do you think it is good news to learn that "God is with us"? Why or why not?

This famous passage about Immanuel is often heard at Christmastime. As a group, can you remember other places in the Bible that God was "with us"? If so, what are they?

Watch [10 MINUTES]

Play the video for this session, which you can access through streaming (see the instructions provided with this guide). Use the following outline to record any thoughts that stand out to you.

Adventures are a lot better when you're doing them with someone.

Jesus, throughout Scripture, has people quitting stuff, and finding stuff, and quitting stuff.

God says that he will never quit us. He's with us, over and over again.

Some doors that are closed are meant to be opened.

Who is somebody that you need to be with and hold close?

Discuss [35 MINUTES]

Discuss what you just watched by answering the following questions.

1. Before everyone shares in the large group, turn to one or two people next to you and finish this sentence: "After watching the video, one question I now have is . . ."

2. Has someone ever said to you, "I'm with you"? If so, how did it affect you? Have you ever said the same words to someone else? If so, what was that like?

3. Bob says that quitting can be a good thing if you "quit the right stuff." Have you ever quit anything? Was the experience positive or negative? What did it make room for in your life?

4. How do you know the right stuff and the wrong stuff to quit?

5. What does it mean that "God will never quit us"? Does that sound like good news or bad news to you?

6. Have you ever had a dream die? Did it die "alone," as Bob says, or were you with anyone? Did being with someone help?

7. Bob makes a distinction between being in a Bible study with someone and just "being" with someone. What's the difference? Is this a helpful distinction? Why or why not?

8. What did you think of Bob's story about Randy? Who has God brought into your life that you can be a "Randy" or "Immanuel" to? To whom do you need to say, "I'm with you"?

Respond [15 MINUTES]

After Bob tells his story about Randy, he challenges you to reach out to someone who has been a "Randy" in your life and tell that person thank you. This is what you're going to do right now. Think about your life. Is there a person who has been there with you when the going got rough? Or a person who poured out his or her life to mentor or counsel you? Or someone who talked you out of making a bad choice or talked you into making a good one? Identify such a person and then, right now, send a text or an email to say thanks. The more immediate this is, the better. Just say, "Thank you for being there for me." Be as specific as you feel comfortable, but practice the risk of gratitude. Afterward, reflect on the following questions.

What was this experience like?

Did you get a response from the person you contacted? If so, what was it?

How has this activity been an example of love "doing" things?

Pray [10 MINUTES]

Close the meeting by praying silently for the person on your left. Pray that each of you will have the courage to "do" the love of Jesus this week, wherever God takes you.

 | # Personal Study

You are invited to further explore the challenge of *Love Does* by engaging in any or all of the following activities between sessions. Remember, this part of *Love Does* is not about following rules or doing your homework. These activities (categorized as *Do*, *Reflect*, and *Read*) are designed to give you the opportunity to jump into the risk of God's kingdom with both feet. As you work through each of these exercises, write down your responses to the questions, as you will be given a few minutes to share your insights at the start of the next session. If you are reading *Love Does* alongside this study, first review the introduction and chapters 1–6 of the book.

 | *Do*: Be a Quitter

In the teaching for this week, Bob told a compelling story about the time he quit high school and made a plan to move to Yosemite National Park to rock climb. Even though that plan did not work out very well, it led to an interesting discipline. Once a week, Bob quits something.

You are invited to do the same this week. Pick something you need to give up (such as texting while you drive or drinking too much coffee in the afternoon) or something you enjoy doing but can put aside for a certain amount of time (such going out for breakfast and lunch, or binge-watching shows in the evening, or scrolling through social media after dinner).

The point in this exercise is that when you choose to quit some of this "old stuff," it makes space for Jesus to bring "new stuff" into your life. So don't rush to fill any new time or emotional space you have with replacement noise, activity, or entertainment. Pay attention in prayer to what Jesus brings into your life so you can say yes to it.

1. What did you decide to quit?

2. Why did you choose to quit this? What was your experience like?

3. Did you find that anything new came into your life through this process?

4. What did you learn about yourself by being a "quitter"? What did you learn about God?

Reflect: Be Salty

For the Reflect sections of this study guide, you will be going through portions of Jesus' epic teaching in Matthew 5–7, also known as the Sermon on the Mount. In this kingdom-of-God manifesto, Jesus gets extremely practical about what it means to live in God's world in God's way and to bring about truth, beauty, and justice as you go. Read the following:

> [13] "You are the salt of the earth. But if the salt loses its saltiness, how can it be made salty again? It is no longer good for anything, except to be thrown out and trampled underfoot.
>
> [14] "You are the light of the world. A town built on a hill cannot be hidden. [15] Neither do people light a lamp and put it under a bowl. Instead they put it on its stand, and it gives light to everyone in the house. [16] In the same way, let your light shine before others, that they may see your good deeds and glorify your Father in heaven."
>
> MATTHEW 5:13–16

Jesus tells his hearers they are the "salt of the earth" (verse 13) and the "light of the world" (verse 14). You may be familiar with some of the background in these two metaphors. In the ancient Near East, salt—more than it was known as a flavoring—was primarily used to dry and preserve meats. Jesus is saying that his followers need to act in ways that preserve and sustain the earth because God's mission is one of healing and restoration—and that healing and restoration includes the creation itself. If the people of God aren't working to sustain that agenda, they are not doing much good and might as well be tossed out.

Furthermore, Jesus claims his people are the light of the world. He draws on the common image of a lamp to describe the way that, like light shining into a dark corner, God's people are supposed to reveal things as they really are. We believe that God's kingdom is here *now* and that things can be here on earth as they are in heaven. This is something we don't simply assert with our lips but actually demonstrate with our lives.

What is so compelling about both of Jesus' metaphors is just how *functional* they are. Jesus seems to expect the faith of his followers will manifest itself in lives of action that are useful to others and positive for the here and now.

1. What else do you think Jesus meant when he talked about being salt and light?

2. What are some of the good ways you have seen Christians be "salty" with their lives and faith? What negative ways have you seen Christians be "salty" with their faith?

3. Is it possible to snuff out your light with the way you try to be salt? Explain your response.

4. Where are you being "salty" in your Christianity? Where do you want to grow?

 | *Read*: Get a New Mindset

In the Read sections of this study guide, you will have the opportunity to reflect on some of the chapters that you've read in *Love Does*. This week, make sure that you read the introduction and chapters 1–6 in the book, and then write down your responses to the following questions.

1. In chapter 2, Bob tells the story of a childhood friend named Dave, who once shot him in the stomach with a pellet gun. Bob writes, "I think it was more about what I saw in Doug than what he had to say to me. In fact, until we were in his room in post-op, we hadn't talked about Jesus much at all." What stands out to you about Dave and the impact his life had on Bob? Who is someone in your life who has made this kind of impact on you?

2. Bob states in chapter 4, "I love those passages in Scripture where Jesus teaches the disciples something, saying, 'I want to teach you to think differently about life.'" How does this statement resonate with you? When has God revealed something to you in his Word that caused you to think differently about your life and about others?

3. Bob relates the story of a painful breakup with his high school sweetheart in chapter 5. He writes, "While painful at the time, I can see now, many years later when I look in the rearview mirror of my life, evidence of God's tremendous love and unfolding adventure for me." What are some things that you can now see—as you likewise look back in the "rearview mirror"—about God's love and the plans he has unfolded in your life?

4. What inspires you about the story in chapter 6 of Bob's persistence in getting into law school? When is a time that someone spoke "words of life" to you?

# Catch Up and Read Ahead

Use this time to go back and complete any of the study and reflection questions from previous studies that you weren't able to finish. Make a note below of any questions you've had and reflect on any growth or personal insights you've gained.

Read chapters 7–12 in *Love Does* before the next group gathering. Use the space below to make note of anything in those chapters that stands out to you or encourages you.

BEFORE GROUP MEETING	Read chapters 7–12 in *Love Does* Read the Welcome section (page 20)
GROUP MEETING	Discuss the Connect questions Read the passage for this session and discuss Watch the video teaching for session 2 Discuss the questions that follow as a group Do the closing exercise and pray (pages 20–24)
STUDY 1: *Do*	Complete the personal study (pages 26–27)
STUDY 2: *Reflect*	Complete the personal study (pages 28–29)
STUDY 3: *Read*	Complete the personal study (page 30)
CATCH UP AND READ AHEAD (BEFORE WEEK 3 GROUP MEETING)	Read chapters 13–18 in *Love Does* Complete any unfinished personal studies (page 31)

Free to Fail

We are no longer defined by our failures. We are defined by Christ.

BOB GOFF

Welcome [READ ON YOUR OWN]

Most people, if they are honest, hate to fail. However, if you asked them why they hate failing, you might not get a great answer. They may say, "Because failing stinks." Agreed. It does. That's obvious. But *why* does it stink? *Why* do we hate to fail?

The reason we hate to fail is the same reason we hate finding awkward pictures of ourselves in old photo albums. It's embarrassing! Failure shakes up the fantasy that we're in control of things and makes us feel vulnerable.

Vulnerability. Now we're getting somewhere.

Feeling vulnerable *is* a scary thing. It's not a place many people want to be. However, it is exactly the place that God so often meets us and changes our lives. Think about it: If everything we did succeeded, we might never learn to trust God at all. And if we're not trusting God, we'll start trusting something else, and then we'll lose our way pretty quickly. However, once we've failed—even just once—and experienced God's love and acceptance in that place of exposure and vulnerability, things start changing.

This week in *Love Does,* you'll explore the nature of failure, how it works, and what God does with it. How have you dealt with failure in the past? Do you handle it well now? Where has God been in your failure? Hang on to those questions as you jump into this session, because maybe your failures are actually opportunities—opportunities to ask not "Who am I now that I've failed?" but "Who is God leading me to become?"

Connect [10 MINUTES]

If you or any of your group members don't know each other, take a few minutes to introduce yourselves. Then discuss the following questions:

- What was your first job? Do you have good memories or bad memories of the experience?

- What is something that resonated with you in last week's personal study that you would like to share with the group?

Read [10 MINUTES]

Ask someone to read the following passage, and then discuss the questions that follow.

¹⁵ When they had finished eating, Jesus said to Simon Peter, "Simon son of John, do you love me more than these?"

"Yes, Lord," he said, "you know that I love you."

Jesus said, "Feed my lambs."

¹⁶ Again Jesus said, "Simon son of John, do you love me?" He answered, "Yes, Lord, you know that I love you."

Jesus said, "Take care of my sheep."

¹⁷ The third time he said to him, "Simon son of John, do you love me?"

Peter was hurt because Jesus asked him the third time, "Do you love me?" He said, "Lord, you know all things; you know that I love you."

Jesus said, "Feed my sheep. ¹⁸ Very truly I tell you, when you were younger you dressed yourself and went where you wanted; but when you are old you will stretch out your hands, and someone else will dress you and lead you where you do not want to go." ¹⁹ Jesus said this to indicate the kind of death by which Peter would glorify God. Then he said to him, "Follow me!"

JOHN 21:15–19

What had Jesus' and Peter's history been before this story? Why do you think Jesus asked Peter the same question three different times?

What does it say about God that Jesus takes Peter back as a disciple? What does it say about Peter that he accepts this reinstatement?

Watch [15 minutes]

Play the video for this session. As you watch, use the following outline to record any thoughts or concepts that stand out to you.

Do you know what it's like to just absolutely, positively, utterly fail? Has that happened to you?

Sometimes God leads us into failure so we'll know about our absolute need for him.

Failures can be opportunities for us to ask, "Who is God leading us into becoming?"

Is our life a series of failures? Or are we becoming refined more into the image of Christ?

Some of us are faking it. We think if people know who we are, they won't like us anymore.

Don't you live somebody else's calling. Live a life worthy of the calling *you've* received.

Failure teaches us about the character of Jesus and who he wants us to be.

Discuss [30 MINUTES]

Discuss what you just watched by answering the following questions.

1. Before everyone shares in the large group, turn to one or two people next to you and finish this sentence, "After watching the video, one question I now have is . . ."

2. Have you ever utterly failed? If so, what happened?

3. Bob states in the video that sometimes God will actually lead us into failures. How do you respond to this statement? Why do you think God would lead us into failures?

4. Bob says, "We are no longer defined by our failures. We are defined by Christ." What does this mean? Do you think it's true? Have you ever experienced it?

5. Bob suggests in the video that because most of us are afraid of failing, we often end up faking it and acting like somebody who isn't us. Have you ever play-acted to be someone you're not? If so, who or what did you pretend to be?

6. What was the result of you play-acting to be someone you're not? What did you learn through the experience?

7. Think about *who* you act like when you're tempted to fake it. What does that image say about what you're afraid of? What does it say about who you are afraid to become?

8. Bob tells a story about posing in a wax museum and suggests that he is a poser when he tries to live into someone else's calling instead of his own. Do you know what your calling is? What are you doing to be faithful to that calling? (If you don't know your calling, brainstorm with the group to determine one step you can take toward discovering it.)

Respond [15 MINUTES]

(For this activity, you will need two nametag stickers.) In the video, Bob mentions that Jesus gave people, such as Peter, nicknames (see Matthew 16:17–19). These nicknames were not based on who the person *used to be* but on who the person *was becoming*. Peter would need to lean into the nickname Jesus gave him—which means *rock*—after the utter failure of his denial of Christ.

In the space provided below, jot down one of your most "epic" fails. It should be a failure that is hard to shake—one that follows you around and causes regret. Be honest, because no one will read this unless you choose to share it.

On one of the nametag stickers, write down a nickname you have given to yourself because of this failure. Now, take a deep breath and write down a nickname on the second sticker you think Jesus would give you based on who you are becoming. Consider: *How are the nicknames different? How are they related? How can you tell when a nickname comes from God and when it comes from elsewhere?*

When everyone is finished, take turns sharing your old nickname. Then, like Bob with his tickets, tear up that nametag and throw it away. (Be as dramatic or subtle as you want.) Once you've thrown away your old nickname, share your new nickname, and then stick that nametag on your shirt. Afterward, reflect on these questions together: What makes for a good "Jesus nickname"? How is it different from the old nickname you were given?

Pray [10 MINUTES]

Close the session by praying together the words that Jesus taught his disciples to pray in the Sermon on the Mount: *"Our Father in heaven, hallowed be your name, your kingdom come, your will be done, on earth as it is in heaven. Give us today our daily bread. And forgive us our debts, as we also have forgiven our debtors. And lead us not into temptation, but deliver us from the evil one"* (Matthew 6:9–13).

 | # Personal Study

In this week's group time, you explored the wonderful freedom that comes from allowing yourself to fail at times. You saw how failures can teach you about your own character and who you want to be, but also how they can teach you about the character of Jesus and who he wants you to be. In this personal study, you will dive deeper into these ideas. As you work through each of these exercises, write down your responses to the questions, as you will be given a few minutes to share your insights at the start of the next session. If you are reading *Love Does* alongside this study, first review chapters 7–12 of the book.

 | *Do*: Fail . . . On Purpose

In the group teaching for this week, Bob talked a bit about how our failures can become opportunities for God to break pieces off of us so there's more for him to work with. In this personal study, you're going to give God some new raw material.

One of the deep, inner dynamics of experiencing the love of God is recognizing when we are in a place of failure and receiving his love right then and there. This is hard to do. When we fail, we want to judge (ourselves or others), get angry, or make excuses to protect our hearts. We end up only doing things we already know we'll be good at so we don't have to experience struggle. But what if, instead, we *intentionally* put ourselves in a place of failure and then practiced keeping our heart open toward God and receiving his love?

Here's how this works. First, think of an activity you know you're not very good at or that is a challenge for you. Some suggestions are listed here, or you can pick your own:

- Take a class at the gym or engage in an exercise you don't normally do.
- Write a poem and read it aloud to another person.
- Dance where others can see you.
- Write a five-minute speech on something that matters to you that you will present to at least two to three other people.
- Other: ____.

Don't choose an activity that could have serious consequences or is foolish (like running a marathon with no training or not finishing a project at work). Once you have determined your activity, pick a time this week, say a prayer, and do it. It will likely be frustrating, difficult, and possibly embarrassing. However, try to stay open to God's love, remember your new "Jesus nickname," and see what happens. Afterward, reflect on this experience by answering the following questions.

1. What was this experience like for you to do?

2. What was your initial impulse when the going got tough?

3. Was it easy or difficult to receive the love of God in the midst of failure? If it was difficult, why do you think that was the case?

4. How might this lesson be transferable to other areas of your life?

 | *Reflect*: Make It Right

Remember that in the Reflect section of each personal study, you will be going through Jesus' epic teaching in the Sermon on the Mount. The following is your reading for this week:

> [21] "You have heard that it was said to the people long ago, 'You shall not murder, and anyone who murders will be subject to judgment.' [22] But I tell you that anyone who is angry with a brother or sister will be subject to judgment. Again, anyone who says to a brother or sister, 'Raca,' is answerable to the court. And anyone who says, 'You fool!' will be in danger of the fire of hell.
>
> [23] "Therefore, if you are offering your gift at the altar and there remember that your brother or sister has something against you, [24] leave your gift there in front of the altar. First go and be reconciled to them; then come and offer your gift.
>
> [25] "Settle matters quickly with your adversary who is taking you to court. Do it while you are still together on the way, or your adversary may hand you over to the judge, and the judge may hand you over to the officer, and you may be thrown into prison. [26] Truly I tell you, you will not get out until you have paid the last penny."

MATTHEW 5:21–26

If you've been around Christianity for a while, you have likely encountered this teaching before. Jesus here expands the boundaries of what it means to love our neighbors as ourselves. In the kingdom of God, it is not sufficient to simply "not kill someone," because God's agenda is much bigger. God wants to heal the root causes of murder: anger, bitterness, the unforgiving human heart—all the dark emotions that gain emotional traction when we tear each other down. This is why Jesus links murder and slander. He is not content to leave us with a gospel of abstinence. Jesus' gospel is a gospel of action.

As the teaching progresses, Jesus exhorts his listeners to go and reconcile with any brother or sister who is holding something against them (see verses 23–24). God's kingdom is about *active goodness* and not just *inactive badness*. This means that healing the human heart takes work—our work as well as the Lord's work. If we want to live out Jesus' way, we will not just avoid slander but also be proactive in making broken relationships whole again.

1. Pray about your own relationships this week. Is God showing you a broken one that needs to be made whole? If so, which one?

2. What is your "next right step" in working with God to heal this relationship? For example, are you willing to be the one who says "I'm sorry" first to get the ball rolling?

3. What would you say scares you the most about doing this exercise?

4. What do you think would happen if you took this step? What, in particular, would you most like to see healed in the relationship with this person?

This week, read through chapters 7–12 in *Love Does*, and then write down your responses to the following questions.

1. Bob writes in chapter 8, "Jesus seemed to say that all we would need to do is to scrape together the pieces of our lives that had fallen on the ground, bring those pieces to him, and he would start using them." How have you seen Jesus use the "broken pieces" in your life? How has he revealed his love to you in a way that made you whole?

2. In chapter 9, Bob relates the events that led to him becoming a diplomat for the Republic of Uganda. He writes, "God sometimes uses the completely inexplicable events in our lives to point us toward him." How have you seen the truth of this statement play out in your life?

3. Bob writes in chapter 11 of one invitation it will kill him to refuse—yet one he is tempted to turn down all the time. What is this invitation? *Living a life of complete engagement.* What does it look like to turn down this kind of invitation to a full life?

4. In chapter 12, Bob tells of the impact a baseball coach made on his young life when he wrote in a card, "Wow . . . what a hit, Bob!" He actually came to believe what the coach had written about him. How has an encouraging word like this made an impact on your life? Who could you likewise reach out to today to extend an encouraging word?

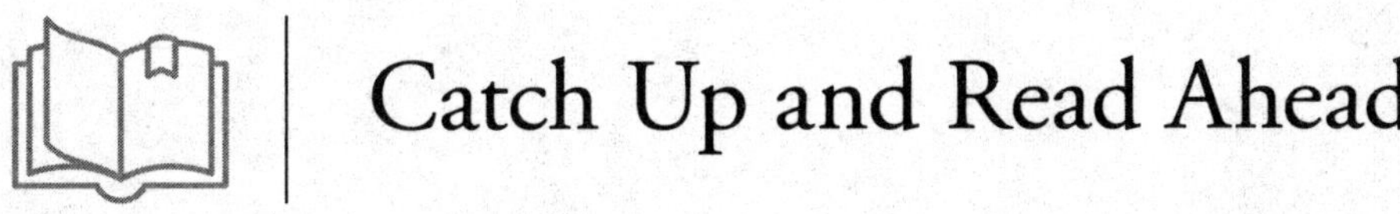

Catch Up and Read Ahead

Use this time to go back and complete any of the study and reflection questions from previous studies that you weren't able to finish. Make a note below of any questions you've had and reflect on any growth or personal insights you've gained.

Read chapters 13–18 in *Love Does* before the next group gathering. Use the space below to make note of anything in those chapters that stands out to you or encourages you.

BEFORE GROUP MEETING	Read chapters 13–18 in *Love Does* Read the Welcome section (page 34)
GROUP MEETING	Discuss the Connect questions Read the passage for this session and discuss Watch the video teaching for session 3 Discuss the questions that follow as a group Do the closing exercise and pray (pages 34–38)
STUDY 1: *Do*	Complete the personal study (pages 40–41)
STUDY 2: *Reflect*	Complete the personal study (pages 42–43)
STUDY 3: *Read*	Complete the personal study (page 44)
CATCH UP AND READ AHEAD (BEFORE WEEK 4 GROUP MEETING)	Read chapters 19–26 in *Love Does* Complete any unfinished personal studies (page 45)

Are we missing that the God of the
universe is nuts about us?

BOB GOFF

Welcome [READ ON YOUR OWN]

If you've ever tried to use a snorkel, you know how tricky it can be. You have to figure out how to keep it upright and learn to swim so the top doesn't dip below the water line. However, if you do get water in your snorkel (which always happens), you get to do the coolest thing: spit it out! That's right—you just shoot water right out the top of your snorkel!

It's kind of fun, but it also has a purpose. You have to clear all that water *out* before you can take your next breath of air *in*. This is because a snorkel is just a tube, and the air you breathe in flows through the same pathway as the air you breathe out. If the top of the snorkel is blocked by water, not only can you not breathe out, but you also cannot breathe in.

The same thing is true with love. The love we have flows from our hearts. Well, not our actual hearts, but from the place that is the center of our being. Our hearts, like the snorkel, are two-way streets. Love flows in and out through the same "tube." This is one of the reasons that Jesus teaches there is a connection between loving God and loving our neighbors. If we are open to loving others, then our hearts are open to being loved by God. And if our hearts are open to being loved by God, then they are free to let love flow to our neighbors.

This week in *Love Does*, the challenge is for you to risk opening parts of your "snorkel" that you may have closed off to the extravagant love of God. You will explore whether it is easier for you to *give* love or receive it—and when that is the case. You will also look at what it might take for you to open yourself to God's love in a brand-new way.

Connect [10 MINUTES]

Start by discussing the following questions as a group:

- What is the biggest favor anyone has ever asked of you?

- What is something that resonated with you in last week's personal study that you would like to share with the group?

Read [10 MINUTES]

Ask someone to read the following passage, and then discuss the questions that follow.

> [7] Let us love one another, for love comes from God. Everyone who loves has been born of God and knows God. [8] Whoever does not love does not know God, because God is love. [9] This is how God showed his love among us: He sent his one and only Son into the world that we might live through him. [10] This is love: not that we loved God, but that he loved us and sent his Son as an atoning sacrifice for our sins. [11] Dear friends, since God so loved us, we also ought to love one another. [12] No one has ever seen God; but if we love one another, God lives in us and his love is made complete in us.
>
> 1 JOHN 4:7–12

What does this passage say about the relationship between God's love and our own?

What does it mean that God's love is "made complete in us" (verse 12)?

Watch [10 MINUTES]

Play the video for this session. As you watch, use the following outline to record any thoughts or concepts that stand out to you.

Have you ever asked something of someone that was so big—so out there—but you didn't even realize how big and how far out there it was because you were so in love?

There is something beautiful that happens when you are so caught up in your love for someone that you want to find new and different ways to express it over and over again.

Have you ever been in a situation where somebody tried to express the kind of love they have for you—the kind of things that have been going on inside of them for so long?

When God was making the earth, did he ever create something and say, "You know what, I can make it better! I want to find new ways to express my love to the people I call my beloved"?

Are we missing out on the fact that the God of the universe is nuts about us?

Discuss [35 MINUTES]

Discuss what you just watched by answering the following questions.

1. Before everyone shares in the large group, turn to one or two people next to you and finish this sentence: "After watching the video, one question I now have is . . ."

2. How did you like Bob's story about Ryan? Did it make you feel more inspired *(I could do that too!)* or condemned *(I've never done anything that creative!)*? Explain your response.

3. What do you learn about God's love from the kind of love that Ryan demonstrated? Is that kind of love easy or hard for you to accept? Explain.

4. Bob suggests there is a difference between trying to "win someone over" and simply "telling them how you feel." Is he right? If so, how do you explain the difference?

5. How do you think this difference might relate to Christian practices such as evangelism?

6. Look again at the passage from 1 John 4:7–12 that you read at the start of the session. Have you ever experienced God's love through the way that someone else in your life treated you? If so, what was that experience like for you?

7. If you have not experienced God's love in that way, what do you think that kind of love *might* look like? What would it look like for you to demonstrate this kind of love to others?

8. Has there ever been a circumstance in your life that God used to show you he loved you? If so, what was it? How could you tell it was God who orchestrated it?

Respond [15 MINUTES]

(For this activity, you will need a way to access YouTube videos.) Bob concludes this week's teaching by asking if we are missing the fact that the God of the universe is crazy about us. This exercise is designed to help you develop eyes to see the activity, presence, and love of God everywhere.

As a group, watch the two or three videos that your leader has selected for you. Nothing is more random than YouTube, so these could range from pop music pieces to kittens playing with socks. Your group leader will have already checked the appropriateness of these videos, so all you have to do is relax and ask yourself this question: *God, where is your kingdom already on display in this video?*

Resist the urge to judge the video's content, morality, or even its technique. This exercise is about developing the skill of locating God's presence in unlikely places. After you are finished, reflect on the following questions together.

What was this experience like for you?

Where did you see God in these videos? Was it hard or easy to find him there?

How might developing this skill you just practiced by watching these videos help you to see God's love more in your everyday life?

Pray [10 MINUTES]

Close by having everyone in the group offer a one-word prayer (yes, just one word!) regarding how you want to experience the love of God this week.

 | # Personal Study

In this week's group time, you explored the audacious love that God has for you. You thought about some of the people he has dropped into your life and some of the opportunities that he has set in your path . . . all because of his great love for you. In this personal study, you will keep exploring God's love and the many ways that he reveals it to you each and every day. As you work through each of these exercises, write down your responses to the questions, as you will be given a few minutes to share your insights at the start of the next session. If you are reading *Love Does* alongside this study, first review chapters 13–18 of the book.

 | *Do*: God Is in This Place

Begin this week's personal study by reading the following story about a man named Jacob:

> ¹⁰ Jacob left Beersheba and set out for Harran. ¹¹ When he reached a certain place, he stopped for the night because the sun had set. Taking one of the stones there, he put it under his head and lay down to sleep. ¹² He had a dream in which he saw a stairway resting on the earth, with its top reaching to heaven, and the angels of God were ascending and descending on it. ¹³ There above it stood the Lord, and he said: "I am the Lord, the God of your father Abraham and the God of Isaac. I will give you and your descendants the land on which you are lying. ¹⁴ Your descendants will be like the dust of the earth, and you will spread out to the west and to the east, to the north and to the south. All peoples on earth will be blessed through you and your offspring. ¹⁵ I am with you and will watch over you wherever you go, and I will bring you back to this land. I will not leave you until I have done what I have promised you."
>
> ¹⁶ When Jacob awoke from his sleep, he thought, "Surely the Lord is in this place, and I was not aware of it." ¹⁷ He was afraid and said, "How awesome is this place! This is none other than the house of God; this is the gate of heaven."
>
> **GENESIS 28:10–17**

One of the surprising things about this story is that Jacob encountered the Lord at a place that no one of the time would have expected. Jacob was not kneeling in a temple, or standing on the top of a mountain, or wading in the waves at the edge of the sea when he had this dream of heaven and earth meeting. Instead, he was literally by the side of the road. A random location. Nowhere special.

Your invitation this week is to likewise seek the presence of God in a place "by the side of the road." This could be a spot you go to often but don't think to look for God there—like the grocery story, or your daughter's dance class, or a work staff meeting, or even the drop-off line at school. Or it could be a place where you don't think about God being present at all—like outside an abortion clinic, or a mall, or your town's version of a "red-light district."

Go to the place you've selected and, if it is safe to do so, walk through and/or around the area. (If it is not, just do this exercise from your car parked nearby or at another location that is safe.) As you do this, pray this prayer: "God, show me where Your kingdom and love are already on display in this place and with these people."* Take care to look everyone you pass in the eye and be friendly. If the temptation to judge creeps up, then pray, "God, help me to think Your thoughts and feel Your feelings for this place and these people."

1. What place did you select? What were your thoughts when you arrived at this location?

2. Where did you find God as you did this activity?

3. Were you surprised to find God there? If so, what surprised you the most?

4. What did you learn about God's love through the process?

* Special thanks to Mark Scandrette and ReIMAGINE for these prayers.

 | *Reflect*: How to Love

The topic of this week's reading in the Sermon on the Mount is the love that we should have for one another. As Jesus explains, God wants us to love even those we consider enemies:

> [43] "You have heard that it was said, 'Love your neighbor and hate your enemy.' [44] But I tell you, love your enemies and pray for those who persecute you, [45] that you may be children of your Father in heaven. He causes his sun to rise on the evil and the good, and sends rain on the righteous and the unrighteous. [46] If you love those who love you, what reward will you get? Are not even the tax collectors doing that? [47] And if you greet only your own people, what are you doing more than others? Do not even pagans do that? [48] Be perfect, therefore, as your heavenly Father is perfect."
>
> MATTHEW 5:43–48

A little background information is needed to understand Jesus' opening words to his listeners: "You have heard that it was said, 'Love your neighbor and hate your enemy'" (verse 43). Jesus delivered his Sermon on the Mount to a primarily *Jewish* audience—a group familiar with the Old Testament. They would have quickly recognized that Jesus was quoting from God's law when he said, "Love your neighbor" (Leviticus 19:18). However, there was no Old Testament passage that advised God's people to "hate" their enemies.

Given this, it appears the reasoning had become that love for one's "neighbor" (fellow Jews) somehow meant that one's "enemies" (non-Jews) could be excluded from that love. It was the classic us-versus-them mentality—love those who are "in" the group but hate those who are deemed "outside" the group. Jesus allowed no such caustic and faulty thinking among his listeners. Rather, he instructed them to love their enemies and even pray for those who were actively *persecuting* them. In this, they could follow the example of their "Father in heaven," who "sends rain on the righteous and the unrighteous" (Matthew 5:45).

Jesus' instruction on how to love God's way applies just as much to us today as it did to the people in the first century. As recipients of God's audacious love, we must be willing to pour that audacious love out to others. There is no "inside" and "outside" when it comes to those we should love. We are to extend God's love to *everyone* in our lives.

1. How do you think this idea of "hating your enemy" developed among people in the first century? How does such an idea develop in our world today?

2. What makes it challenging for you to love your "enemies"—those you don't get along with?

3. What is the problem in only loving those who love you?

4. How can remembering the audacious love and mercy that God has shown toward you help you to likewise show audacious love and mercy toward others?

This week, read through chapters 13–18 in *Love Does*, and then write down your responses to the following questions.

1. Think about the game of Bigger and Better that Bob describes in chapter 13. What are some of the things you've released to God? How did he give you something better in return?

2. Bob writes in chapter 15, "Faith isn't an equation or a formula or a business deal that gets you what you want. In short, there's nothing on the other side of the equals sign, just Jesus." How do you respond to this idea when you consider your faith?

3. Bob writes in chapter 17 of a time as a boy when he came up one penny short to buy some candy. The storekeeper polished up one of the pennies he did have and made a special rule just for him: *Shiny pennies are worth two.* We each get to be like this storekeeper when it comes to deciding that people, including ourselves, are worth more than others might figure. Who is someone who needs you to extend this kind of "rule" to them? What steps will you take this week to let that person know what his or her worth is to you?

4. Consider this statement from chapter 18: "You become like the people you hang around, and to a great degree, you end up going wherever they're headed." Who are the people you hang around? Are they taking you in the direction that you want to go, or do you think they might be taking you in the wrong direction? Explain your thoughts.

# Catch Up and Read Ahead

Use this time to go back and complete any of the study and reflection questions from previous studies that you weren't able to finish. Make a note below of any questions you've had and reflect on any growth or personal insights you've gained.

Read chapters 19–26 in *Love Does* before the next group gathering. Use the space below to make note of anything in those chapters that stands out to you or encourages you.

BEFORE GROUP MEETING	Read chapters 19–26 in *Love Does* Read the Welcome section (page 48)
GROUP MEETING	Discuss the Connect questions Read the passage for this session and discuss Watch the video teaching for session 4 Discuss the questions that follow as a group Do the closing exercise and pray (pages 48–52)
STUDY 1: *Do*	Complete the personal study (pages 54–55)
STUDY 2: *Reflect*	Complete the personal study (pages 56–57)
STUDY 3: *Read*	Complete the personal study (page 58)
CATCH UP AND READ AHEAD (BEFORE WEEK 5 GROUP MEETING)	Read chapters 27–31 in *Love Does* Complete any unfinished personal studies (page 59)

 | # Be Not Afraid

Welcome [READ ON YOUR OWN]

In 1975, the movie *Jaws* broke box office records and was hailed as one of the summer's blockbusters. However, as celebrated as the movie was for its domestic gross earnings, great performances, and iconic score, *Jaws* was famous for another reason as well.

The film's antagonist, a motorized replica of a great white shark, kept breaking down during production. Because of this, the film's director, Steven Spielberg, had to shoot "around" the shark, implying its presence in scenes while never directly showing it to the audience. But instead of making the movie worse, it made it better! Not being able to see what the heroes were hunting built such suspense and dread that once the shark was finally on screen—out in the light—it was actually a relief. Once you could see it, it was not nearly as intimidating.

The same is true of the things that scare us today. Our fears have power over us when they are kept in the dark. Their hiddenness fuels all sorts of shame and humiliation in our lives and drives us to make bad decisions. However, when we name our fears and speak them aloud—especially to someone else—the God of the universe can dispel them with the light of his love. Just like the shark in *Jaws*, our fears become less scary once they are out in the open.

This is a bit of what we will do this week in *Love Does*. What are you afraid of? Are there fears that keep you locked up inside? Is there an anxiety that keeps you from acting and chasing after what Jesus is calling you to? Do you think addressing those fears head-on, exposing them, and maybe even laughing about them would give God a context to bring freedom into your life? After all, there is a reason God so frequently says "Don't be afraid" in the Bible. It's because we don't have to be. Fear, in many respects, is a choice—and when we lean on our Creator and entrust ourselves to his love, we find the things we fear most are not so scary after all.

Connect [10 MINUTES]

Start by discussing the following questions as a group:

- What is one thing you were scared of as a child that you're not scared of today?

- What is something that resonated with you in last week's personal study that you would like to share with the group?

Read [10 MINUTES]

Ask someone to read the following passage, and then discuss the questions that follow.

45 Immediately Jesus made his disciples get into the boat and go on ahead of him to Bethsaida, while he dismissed the crowd. 46 After leaving them, he went up on a mountainside to pray.

47 Later that night, the boat was in the middle of the lake, and he was alone on land. 48 He saw the disciples straining at the oars, because the wind was against them. Shortly before dawn he went out to them, walking on the lake. He was about to pass by them, 49 but when they saw him walking on the lake, they thought he was a ghost. They cried out, 50 because they all saw him and were terrified.

Immediately he spoke to them and said, "Take courage! It is I. Don't be afraid." 51 Then he climbed into the boat with them, and the wind died down. They were completely amazed, 52 for they had not understood about the loaves; their hearts were hardened.

MARK 6:45–52

What does this story mean to you when it comes to your fears?

What reassurance does this story provide that Jesus will meet you in your fears?

Watch [15 MINUTES]

Play the video for this session. As you watch, use the following outline to record any thoughts or concepts that stand out to you.

There are those places in our lives where the pace slows down and we can think about things.

Jesus knew what it was like to live a really full life—and then to give that to somebody else.

Fear can lure us away from living the big adventure that God has for us.

Jesus wants us to do a "cannonball"—to go all in on life.

Scripture points us to Jesus. Fellow Christians also point us to Jesus.

Sometimes we think, If I really go on this adventure, I'm going to crash and burn along the way. Meanwhile, heaven is saying, "No, you won't. You're a child of God."

What are you holding on to? What are you afraid is going to happen if you let go? Untie your boat. Get back to building that rocket ship that was your life.

Discuss [30 MINUTES]

Discuss what you just watched by answering the following questions.

1. Before everyone shares in the large group, turn to one or two people next to you and finish this sentence: "After watching the video, one question I now have is . . ."

2. Bob uses the phrase "live a full life." What do you think makes a life "full"?

3. Adam saw in the boat the potential for adventure. He also saw that same potential in his life. How do you see your life? Is there a potential for adventure? Why or why not?

4. When is the last time that you've said "let's go now" when it came to taking a risk? A time when you didn't have a plan or a "chart" for your next move?

5. What things draw you away from "magnetic north"—away from the life that God wants you to have? Why do you think those things tend to draw you away?

6. What is the difference between being brave and being foolish when it comes to stepping out to trust God? How do you distinguish between them?

7. Bob notes that in "dead reckoning," you take a couple of fixed points to determine where you are. You can do the same in your life by drawing a "line" from Scripture to yourself and by drawing a "line" from wise people (who point you toward Jesus) to yourself. How have the Bible and the wise people in your world helped you to "find yourself"? How have you benefited from both the Bible and the wisdom of other followers of Jesus?

8. Think about your life as a "boat." Where would you say it is in relation to the "dock"? Is it tied tightly? If so, what would help you untie the boat so you could sail freely?

Respond [15 MINUTES]

Now that we have discussed the power of spontaneously stepping into adventure with God, we are going to practice this posture with a classic group game: the human knot.

Divide into groups of six to eight people. Stand in a tight circle and place your hands into the center. Grab the hand of someone across from you in the circle (if possible, do not grab the hand of the person immediately next to you). Once everyone is holding two other hands, you have ten minutes to "untie" the knot without letting go of each other. When you are done, the group should be in a circle. You might want to sit this one out—but don't! Practice seeing the possibility for adventure in this activity rather than refusing to do something you don't like.

When your knot is untied, or ten minutes are up, reflect on the following questions.

What was it like for you to have to just jump into the game?

On a scale of fun to annoying, where did this activity land for you? Why?

How does practicing adventure work against fear in our lives?

Pray [10 MINUTES]

Close the session by reciting the following Collect from the Book of Common Prayer: *"O God our King, by the resurrection of your Son Jesus Christ on the first day of the week, you conquered sin, put death to flight, and gave us the hope of everlasting life: Redeem all our days by this victory; forgive our sins, banish our fears, make us bold to praise you and to do your will; and steel us to wait for the consummation of your kingdom on the last great Day; through the same Jesus Christ our Lord. Amen."*

 | # Personal Study

This week's group time was all about facing down your fears and stepping into the life of adventure that God has for you. He doesn't want you to just put your toe in the water. He wants you to do a cannonball—to grab your knees and go all in! This is what you will "dive" into in this personal study. As you work through the exercises, continue to write down your responses, as you will be given time to share your insights at the start of the next session. If you are reading *Love Does* alongside this study, first review chapters 19–26 of the book.

 | *Do*: Welcome a Stranger

The author of the book of Hebrews writes these important words about the importance of hospitality: "Keep on loving one another as brothers and sisters. Do not forget to show hospitality to strangers, for by so doing some people have shown hospitality to angels without knowing it. Continue to remember those in prison as if you were together with them in prison, and those who are mistreated as if you yourselves were suffering" (13:1–3).

Behind some of our most primal fears is often a basic fear of the unknown. The unfamiliar or unseen is usually scariest to us. This is why one of the classic Christian disciplines that can heal our fear is the practice of hospitality. Through hospitality—welcoming strangers (or the unknown) into our home, reaching out to the sick and needy—we turn our fear into friendship and do another small part in bringing heaven to earth.

This week, you are invited to welcome a stranger in one of three ways.

First, you can have a meal with a "stranger." This can represent anything from buying lunch for and eating with a person living on the streets who is in need to inviting some new neighbors over for dinner. Ask God to show you which stranger to welcome.

Second, you can visit someone who is sick.

Third, you can go to someone in need. Is there someone in the hospital or a shut-in you could call on? Is there someone in prison you could visit or write a letter to? Again, ask God to show you someone already in your life orbit to whom you might extend hospitality. Choose one of these three ideas—and then act!

1. Which way of welcoming a stranger did you choose? Why that particular option?

2. What did you learn about yourself and about God through this exercise?

3. What was the hardest part about doing this exercise? Why?

4. Would living this way more often make you less afraid? Why or why not?

 | *Reflect*: Go Down to the Water

The topic of this week's reading in the Sermon on the Mount is about trusting God to take care of our needs. As Jesus explains, he does not want us to be anxious about our lives:

> [25] "Therefore I tell you, do not worry about your life, what you will eat or drink; or about your body, what you will wear. Is not life more than food, and the body more than clothes? [26] Look at the birds of the air; they do not sow or reap or store away in barns, and yet your heavenly Father feeds them. Are you not much more valuable than they? [27] Can any one of you by worrying add a single hour to your life?
>
> [28] "And why do you worry about clothes? See how the flowers of the field grow. They do not labor or spin. [29] Yet I tell you that not even Solomon in all his splendor was dressed like one of these. [30] If that is how God clothes the grass of the field, which is here today and tomorrow is thrown into the fire, will he not much more clothe you—you of little faith? [31] So do not worry, saying, 'What shall we eat?' or 'What shall we drink?' or 'What shall we wear?' [32] For the pagans run after all these things, and your heavenly Father knows that you need them. [33] But seek first his kingdom and his righteousness, and all these things will be given to you as well. [34] Therefore do not worry about tomorrow, for tomorrow will worry about itself. Each day has enough trouble of its own."

MATTHEW 6:25–34

Jesus moves toward the conclusion of this grand teaching in Matthew's Gospel with an actual command not to worry. Taken out of context, this can feel like an unachievable demand. *Don't worry? Are you crazy, Jesus? I have no control over that—and now I'm worried I can't live up to your expectation not to worry!*

Relax. This is not what Jesus is getting at. There is a flow to the Sermon on the Mount. It's going somewhere. Jesus' command not to worry appears at the conclusion of a long section about entrusting ourselves to God. God is trustworthy, Jesus explains, and the more we accept that truth and practice it, the freer we become from worry and anxiety.

Bob began the teaching for this week by talking about how he likes to be "down by the water," because for him it is there that life slows down and its relentless cadence is disrupted. So, your invitation is to take this meditation and find some water to sit beside. It can be the ocean, a lake, a river, a swimming pool, or a decorative fountain. Wherever you go, let the water symbolize the place where life slows down for a bit.

Once you arrive at your destination, take a few deep breaths and practice just being with God. You can reflect on where your life is with God and where he wants to take you next. Or you might consider your fears—where they come from and what it will take to surrender them to God. Whatever you do, don't fill this time by the water with activity. Too much activity (even if it's good stuff like reading the Bible) can actually rob you of the benefits of resting. Take the time to just *be*. Once you've returned from the water's edge, reflect on the experience.

1. Where did you choose to go? How long did you stay there?

2. How would you describe the experience in one word?

3. Did anything distract you while you were alone? Did that tell you anything about yourself?

4. How could a practice like this be part of your everyday life with God?

 | *Read*: Be Real

This week, read through chapters 19–26 in *Love Does*, and then write down your responses to the following questions.

1. Bob tells the story in chapter 19 of an elderly woman named Lynn running into him on the road—literally. After the accident, Lynn couldn't believe that Bob had forgiven her. What lesson did Bob say he learned about God from this experience? Why do you think it is often so hard for us to believe that God has really forgiven us for our mistakes?

2. Bob says in chapter 21, "Human beings are limited [but] God isn't limited at all. He can communicate to us in any way he wants to anytime he wants to." What are some of the ways you've heard God speak to you? What makes listening to him hard for you?

3. When Bob bought a valuable painting called *The Puppeteer*, as told in chapter 22, the art dealer also gave him a fake version of the work. The idea was to hang the counterfeit version on the wall and keep the valuable piece locked up safe. How are we often tempted to do the same when it comes to presenting our real selves to the world?

4. Bob writes in chapter 26, "What I've learned the more time I've spent following Jesus is that God delights in answering our impossible prayers." What are some "impossible" prayers you've seen God answer? How has that encouraged you to pray even bolder prayers?

# Catch Up and Read Ahead

Use this time to go back and complete any of the study and reflection questions from previous studies that you weren't able to finish. Make a note below of any questions you've had and reflect on any growth or personal insights you've gained.

Read chapters 27–31 in *Love Does* before the next group gathering. Use the space below to make note of anything in those chapters that stands out to you or encourages you.

BEFORE GROUP MEETING	Read chapters 27–31 in *Love Does* Read the Welcome section (page 62)
GROUP MEETING	Discuss the Connect questions Read the passage for this session and discuss Watch the video teaching for session 5 Discuss the questions that follow as a group Do the closing exercise and pray (pages 62–66)
STUDY 1: *Do*	Complete the personal study (page 68)
STUDY 2: *Reflect*	Complete the personal study (pages 69–70)
STUDY 3: *Read*	Complete the personal study (page 71)
WRAP IT UP	Connect with someone in your group (page 72) Complete any unfinished personal studies Connect with your group about the next study that you want to go through together

Follow Me

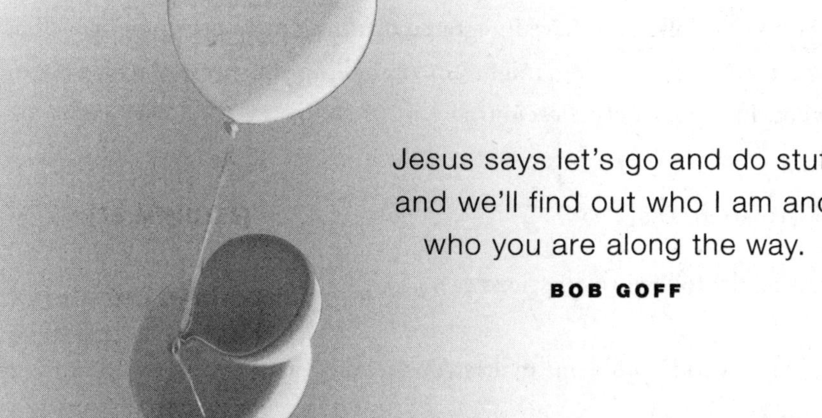

Jesus says let's go and do stuff
and we'll find out who I am and
who you are along the way.

BOB GOFF

Welcome [READ ON YOUR OWN]

Once upon a time, there were two pilgrims going on a road trip with some friends. Pilgrim A was the kind of person who wanted to have every stop mapped out ahead of time. He always picked the most direct route (so he would arrive at his destination on schedule), and any sightseeing was planned in advance (nothing spontaneous).

Pilgrim B, however, was happy to just go with the flow. It didn't matter when and where the group stopped, ate, or arrived. Nor did she care what route they took. And if some interesting attraction came up along the way, she gladly detoured the whole caravan to see it.

When Jesus invites us to follow him, he doesn't tell us every step of the journey ahead. There are adventures and discoveries awaiting us that we could never anticipate. However, this doesn't mean we should never make a plan. In fact, when we read the Gospels, it seems as if Jesus looks for disciples who start with the passion of Pilgrim B and then adopt the practicality of Pilgrim A. He is looking for people with enough enthusiasm to abandon their vocations to follow him, yet he expects those disciples to mature into women and men who can be intentional about bringing God's kingdom here and now.

As the Gospel stories progress, we start to see why. Jesus' intention isn't to stick around. His plan is to leave and turn everything over to his disciples with the guidance of the Holy Spirit to show them the next steps.

In this final session of *Love Does*, you will explore how to bring your passions and plans together. Do you know folks who have integrated planning into their praying? What did that look like? Furthermore, what, if anything, might God be calling you to make a plan about? Consider all of this as you conclude your *Love Does* journey.

Connect [10 MINUTES]

Start by discussing the following questions as a group:

- Which of the world's problems makes you feel the most overwhelmed because it is so big and complicated?

- What is something that resonated with you in last week's personal study that you would like to share with the group?

Read [10 MINUTES]

Ask different people in the group to read aloud the following passages, and then discuss the questions that follow.

[18] As Jesus was walking beside the Sea of Galilee, he saw two brothers, Simon called Peter and his brother Andrew. They were casting a net into the lake, for they were fishermen. [19] "Come, follow me," Jesus said, "and I will send you out to fish for people." [20] At once they left their nets and followed him.

MATTHEW 4:18–20

Then Jesus said to his disciples, "Whoever wants to be my disciple must deny themselves and take up their cross and follow me."

MATTHEW 16:24

[18] A certain ruler asked him, "Good teacher, what must I do to inherit eternal life?"

[19] "Why do you call me good?" Jesus answered. "No one is good—except God alone. [20] You know the commandments: 'You shall not commit adultery, you shall not murder, you shall not steal, you shall not give false testimony, honor your father and mother.'"

[21] "All these I have kept since I was a boy," he said.

[22] When Jesus heard this, he said to him, "You still lack one thing. Sell everything you have and give to the poor, and you will have treasure in heaven. Then come, follow me."

LUKE 18:18–22

What are two or three things that these passages have in common?

In each case, following Jesus means leaving one thing behind for something better. What might Jesus be asking you to leave behind today in order to better follow him?

Watch [10 MINUTES]

Play the video for this session. As you watch, use the following outline to record any thoughts or concepts that stand out to you.

Get anywhere that God's people are—where the hurting are—and just jump in.

Jesus invites us to follow him, but often we instead just keep waving to him.

People who are not just waving at Jesus—who are truly connected to him—look at the needs in the world and say, "There's just got to be more that we can do."

God wants to blow our minds with how good he is.

What if we just said to others, "I am available"? What if we were inefficient with our love—and our goal was to be more and more inefficient with it as time went by?

Discuss [30 MINUTES]

Discuss what you just watched by answering the following questions.

1. Before everyone shares in the large group, turn to one or two people next to you and finish this sentence: "After watching the video, one question I now have is . . ."

2. Bob tells the story of how he was waving at the kids running after his jeep in Uganda. He thought he was saying "hi," but in that culture, the gesture meant "follow me." He notes, "I think Jesus has been doing that to me. He says, 'Bob, follow me.' And I keep waving to him, saying, 'hi.'" How does this resonate with you? When are some times that you have just been waving "hi" at Jesus when he is asking you to follow him?

3. Bob states, "Jesus loves justice." What is justice? What does God's justice look like?

4. In the video, Bob challenges us to consider making a difference for God. A big difference, not a small difference! How does this challenge to dream big effect you? Is it invigorating or intimidating, or a little of both? Explain.

5. Bob asks, "What if we're the ones who aren't efficient with our love?" What do you think he means by this question? Are you too efficient with your love? Or not efficient enough?

6. Jesus doesn't screen our calls! He is always available and ready to just talk with us. What would it look like if followers of Jesus made themselves available in this way?

7. Bob asks, "What if we're the ones who aren't efficient with our love?" What do you think he means by this question? Are you too efficient with your love? Or not efficient enough?

8. What is an area of your life where you sense that God is asking you to stop "waving" at him and start doing something for him? What steps will you take in the weeks and months ahead to actually take God up on this offer, step out, and do what he is calling you to do?

Respond [20 MINUTES]

(For this activity, you will need access to a laptop computer or just your phone.) For the past four weeks, you have engaged in practical activities after the discussion time that are designed to help you put love into action. This week, it's *your* turn to provide the activities.

One of the questions you had the opportunity to discuss during this week's check-in time was about which of the world's problems makes you feel the most overwhelmed. During the video, Bob then challenged you to follow the lead of his friend John and consider what your "Two Bunk" caper might be. Now you will mash these two ideas together: where God's people are hurting in the world and what your next move could be to do something about it.

For the next ten minutes, use one of the laptop computers or your cell phone to research the problem you described as overwhelming. Make notes below on the size and scope of the problem as well as anything you discover about how to help. Then cook up the biggest, most audacious scheme you can think of to help be part of the solution to this problem.

My research and my plan:

Now take five minutes to go around the group and share about both the problem and your solution. Then, as a group, brainstorm what each person's "next step" can be. The goal is for each group member to leave with at least one concrete action that he or she can take to live out a life where "love does." (And if you have trouble thinking of a "next step," give Bob a call. His number is in the back of the *Love Does* book!)

My next step:

Pray [10 MINUTES]

Close the same way you did in session 1: by praying silently for the person on your left. Pray for the courage to "do" the love of Jesus as each of you leaves this place and goes wherever God leads.

 | # Personal Study

Congratulations! You've taken up the challenge to put God's love into action and have now completed the study. Along the way, you've discovered what it means to take risks in demonstrating the audacious love of God to the people in your world—and to the people in the world at large. In this final personal study, you will explore some final ways that you can "hear and do." As you work through each of these exercises, continue to journal your responses. If you are reading *Love Does* alongside this study, first review chapters 27–31 of the book.

The "Do" challenge for this week is to follow up on the next step you envisioned with your group. This is part of the grand adventure you are invited to join when you follow Jesus! So don't pay your discipleship via lip service only. Get out there this week and take that next step! Once you have, use the following prompts to journal about the experience.

1. What I ended up actually doing for my next step:

2. The obstacles I faced, if any, in taking this next step:

3. How this step of demonstrating God's love was received:

Once you have taken this step, send your group members a text or email to let them know how it went. Then start scheming for where God might be leading you to go next!

 | *Reflect*: Hear and Do

Complete your time in the Sermon on the Mount by reading the following passage:

> [24] "Therefore everyone who hears these words of mine and puts them into practice is like a wise man who built his house on the rock. [25] The rain came down, the streams rose, and the winds blew and beat against that house; yet it did not fall, because it had its foundation on the rock. [26] But everyone who hears these words of mine and does not put them into practice is like a foolish man who built his house on sand. [27] The rain came down, the streams rose, and the winds blew and beat against that house, and it fell with a great crash."
>
> MATTHEW 7:24–27

As you have seen in these Reflect sections, Jesus' "kingdom manifesto," the Sermon on the Mount, has a flow. It's not a collection of disconnected proverbs but a train that's headed somewhere. This destination is found in the passage you just read.

Jesus has been inviting his hearers to fully entrust themselves to God and his way of living. The kind of life Jesus describes is how humans were created to live and where they will find life, hope, justice, and peace. However, he warns this way of life is not easy.

Sometimes we get the impression (or are explicitly taught) that if we just keep close enough to Jesus on the narrow path, everything will work out okay—that we will be immune from suffering and get a pass on tragedy. Sadly, nothing could be further from the truth. Storms, as Jesus points out, will come. They are unavoidable. They are the stuff of life. Everyone will encounter them. The difference is where we choose to "build our house."

Jesus says that if we put his teachings into practice (or, in other words, become his followers), we will be like a house built on the rock. When life's storms batter us, we will have the inner strength to stand firm against the wind and rain. And when the sun comes out again, we will still be standing—because we trust the Son. Do you believe it?

1. When you consider Jesus' call to follow him, how much do you think about the storms?

2. Do you think there are any storms that are more than you and God could handle? Explain.

3. What does a "house built on sand" look like? Why doesn't it hold up in a storm?

4. Take a moment to consider how you have been building your life "on the rock" as you have gone through this study.

Because of my *Love Does* experience, I used to think ___________________________________,
but now I know ____.

The best thing about this *Love Does* experience was _______________________________.
The worst thing was ____.

If I could describe my *Love Does* experience in one word, it would be: ____________________
____.

 | *Read*: Put It into Practice

This week, read through chapters 27–31 in *Love Does*, and then write down your responses to the following questions.

1. Bob writes in chapter 27, "What whimsy means to me is a combination of the 'do' part of faith along with doing something worth doing." What does *whimsy* mean to you? What are some examples of how *whimsy* plays out in your life and in your faith?

2. Think about the statement made in chapter 28 that Jesus never said *not* to have disputes; he just said there is a small list of things actually worth having a dispute about. What are some of the things that you believe are worth standing up for?

3. Bob writes in chapter 29, "I can't think of a single time where Jesus asked his friends to just agree with him." Agreeing wasn't enough . . . Jesus wanted them to go out and *do*. What steps are you taking to not just *study* God's Word but actually put it into *practice*?

4. As Bob notes in chapter 30, there is really nothing you can lose in this life if you have Jesus. How has this truth helped you to live "palms up" when it comes to being vulnerable?

Wrap It Up

Use this time to go back and complete any of the study and reflection questions from previous days that you weren't able to finish. Make note of what God has revealed to you in these days. Finally, talk with your group about what study you may want to go through next. Put a date on the calendar for when you'll meet next to study God's Word and dive deeper into community.

EVERYBODY ALWAYS

BECOMING LOVE *in a* WORLD FULL *of* SETBACKS *and* DIFFICULT PEOPLE

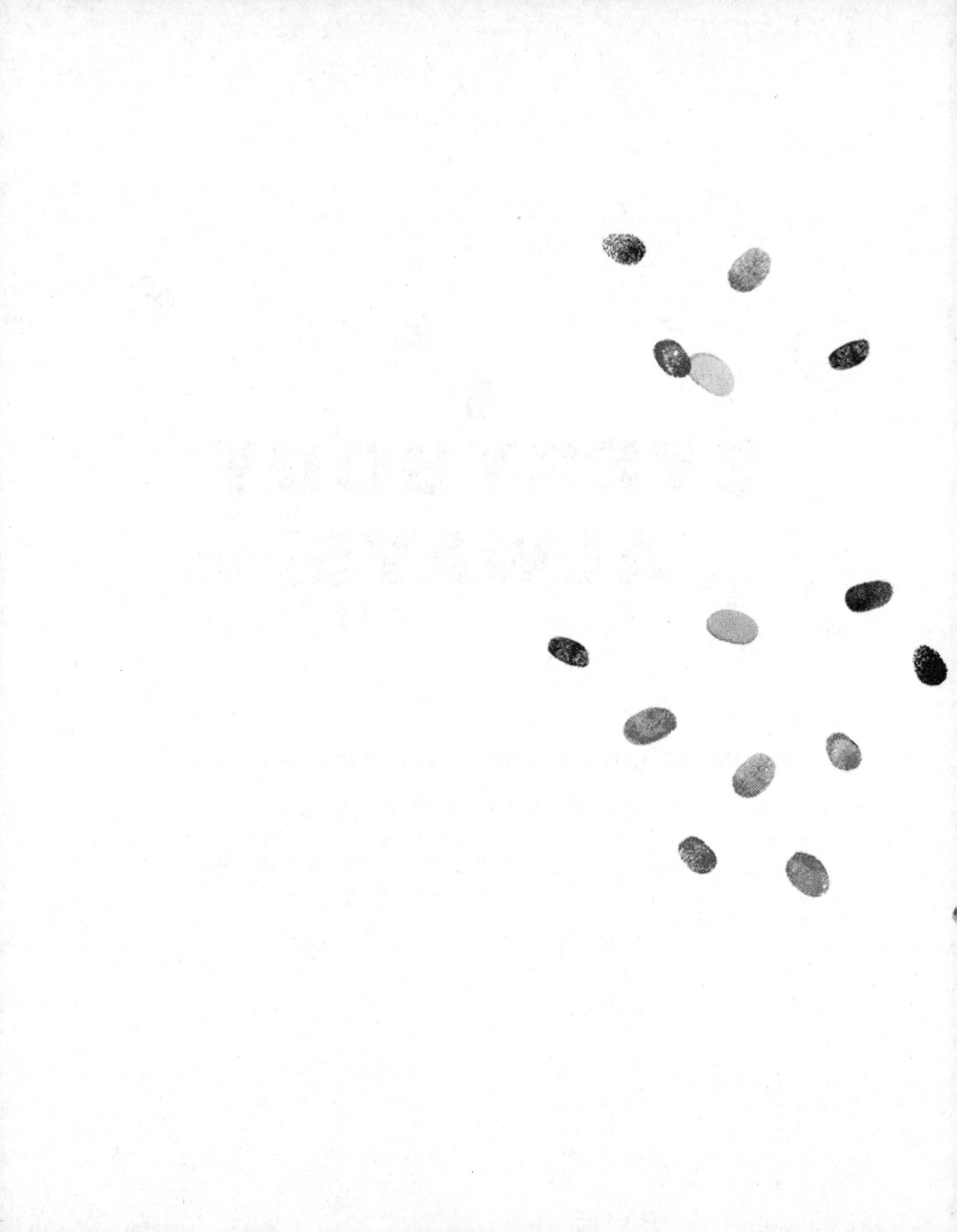

A Note from Bob

Welcome to *Everybody, Always*!

It's good that you're here. Like, really good. Because the world we're living in right now is really good at something else: division. It is great at teaching us to only trust people who talk like us, think like us, vote like us, live where we do, and see everything like we do. And it also teaches us that anybody who talks, thinks, votes, worships, or sees the world differently than us can't be trusted. They may even be our enemy. This way of seeing the world makes love pretty conditional—with the condition being, *we only have to love people who are just like us.*

The good news is that God isn't like that. Not even close. God's love is unconditional, and it's for everybody. God's love turns enemies into friends, and it is bigger than all the things we cook up to divide ourselves. But God doesn't want to be the only one around here who loves this way. He wants us to love this way too. You see, God doesn't want us to love some people, sometimes. He wants us to love everybody, always.

Everybody? Yes, everybody. The people we like and the people we don't? Yes. The people we respect and the people who creep us out? Exactly. The people we admire and the people we don't? Them too. Everybody actually means *everybody*.

Well, what about *always*? Does that mean, literally, always? Yes, it does. As in, when we feel like it and when we don't? Yep. When it's easy and when it's hard? Bingo. When it gives us energy and when it wears us out? Precisely. For God, always really means *always*.

Now, if this sounds like a tall order, you're right. But you're also in luck. God does not leave us to love this way by trusting in our own willpower. The Holy Spirit is around to actually help us love this way. But there's another part too: This is something we can actually train in to get better. Like running a marathon or practicing an instrument, love is something we learn and grow in as we practice.

And that's where a study like this comes in really handy.

Bob Goff

BEFORE GROUP MEETING	Read the prologue and chapters 1–3 in *Everybody, Always* Read the Welcome section (page 78)
GROUP MEETING	Discuss the Connect questions Read the passage for this session and discuss Watch the video teaching for session 1 Discuss the questions that follow as a group Do the closing exercise and pray (pages 78–83)
STUDY 1: *Do*	Complete the personal study (pages 86–87)
STUDY 2: *Reflect*	Complete the personal study (pages 88–89)
STUDY 3: *Read*	Complete the personal study (page 90)
CATCH UP AND READ AHEAD (BEFORE WEEK 2 GROUP MEETING)	Read chapters 4–6 in *Everybody, Always* Complete any unfinished personal studies (page 91)

Love People Where You Are

We don't need to cross the ocean
to love people extravagantly, we
just need to cross the street.

BOB GOFF

Welcome [READ ON YOUR OWN]

You've probably heard of the musical *Wicked*. It was a big deal when it premiered in 2003, winning all the awards there were to win. It was then released as a motion picture in 2024, winning even more awards and grossing millions of dollars. So, why was it so popular? Aside from amazing songs and great performances, *Wicked* took the story of *The Wizard of Oz* and did something unexpected.

In *Wicked*, the familiar story of Dorothy is retold from the perspective of Elphaba Thropp, better known as the Wicked Witch of the West. In this telling, we learn about Elphaba's sad backstory, the rivalry with her sister (Glinda the Good Witch), and how she might not be the one-dimensional villain we thought she was. The musical presents us with an Elphaba who is more misunderstood than mean. It also shows us that when you learn someone's story, it can change how you see that person.

In our culture, it's tempting to sift everybody into two categories: "good guys" and "bad guys." But that's not real life, is it? Real life is way more interesting than that. Everybody we know is a fully formed, complex, and interesting creation. Nobody in our orbit is all good or all bad. Learning people's stories helps us see this. It breaks down our judgments and preconceived notions. It frees us from viewing others as cardboard cutouts but instead as the actual, real, God-created people they are. And, like Elphaba, learning someone's story might help us see them in a different light.

When you get caught up in a life of following Jesus, the old categories of "good guys" and "bad guys" stop working for you. You realize that not only does everybody have a story, but also that God wants us to love them too: *no matter what*. Yes, this can be kind of scary, but that's why we learn people's stories. It makes the creepy people God wants us to love a lot less scary and frees us to actually reach out to them right where they are. All this is what we're talking about this week in our first session of *Everybody, Always*. We're going to share some stories, learn to reach out to our neighbors, and figure out how to actually love everybody God has already put in our lives . . . always.

Connect [10 MINUTES]

If you or any of your group members don't know each other, take a few minutes to introduce yourselves. Then discuss the following questions:

- If you could describe your expectations for this study in one word, what would that word be?

- Why did you pick the word you did?

Read [10 MINUTES]

Ask someone to read the following passage, and then discuss the questions that follow.

25 On one occasion an expert in the law stood up to test Jesus. . . . "Teacher," he asked, "what must I do to inherit eternal life?"

26 "What is written in the Law?" he replied. "How do you read it?"

27 He answered, "'Love the Lord your God with all your heart and with all your soul and with all your strength and with all your mind'; and, 'Love your neighbor as yourself.'"

28 "You have answered correctly," Jesus replied. "Do this and you will live."

29 But he wanted to justify himself, so he asked Jesus, "And who is my neighbor?"

30 In reply Jesus said: "A man was going down from Jerusalem to Jericho, when he was attacked by robbers. They stripped him of his clothes, beat him and went away, leaving him half dead. 31 A priest happened to be going down the same road, and when he saw the man, he passed by on the other side. 32 So too, a Levite, when he came to the place and saw him, passed by on the other side.33 But a Samaritan, as he traveled, came where the man was; and when he saw him, he took pity on him. 34 He went to him and bandaged his wounds, pouring on oil and wine. Then he put the man on his own donkey, brought him to an inn and took care of him. 35 The next day he took out two denarii and gave them to the innkeeper. 'Look after him,' he said, 'and when I return, I will reimburse you for any extra expense you may have.'

36 "Which of these three do you think was a neighbor to the man who fell into the hands of robbers?"

37 The expert in the law replied, "The one who had mercy on him." Jesus told him, "Go and do likewise."

LUKE 10:25-37

At the end of this parable, Jesus asks the teacher of the law which of the three people who passed the half-dead man on the road was a "neighbor" to him (see verse 36). Why does Jesus ask this question? Why do you think the expert in the law answers the way he does?

Have you ever seen someone give away extravagant love to a person who was their enemy? If so, when was it and what did it look like?

Watch [20 MINUTES]

Play the video for this session. As you watch, use the following outline to record any thoughts or concepts that stand out to you.

Let the people in your life know that they are not only *invited* but also *welcome*.

You do business with *buyers*, but you do life with *neighbors*.

Loving your neighbors is woven into your DNA and your faith.

God's message to you is that you don't have to be afraid anymore.

God gives you a peek at what he is doing in the world through the people around you.

Part of finding your joy in life is helping others find their joy.

God wants you to love everyone, but what you need to do is start across the street.

What's a next big step for you? Who are you going to get to know? What is your next courageous move?

Discuss [30 MINUTES]

Discuss what you just watched by answering the following questions.

1. In the video, Bob talks about how he was looking for a *neighbor* rather than just a *buyer* for his house because you "do life" with a neighbor. What does it mean to "do life" with someone? What's an example of this in your life?

2. Do you feel as if you truly "know" your neighbors or just "know about" them? Explain.

3. When you think about your neighbors, what is the hardest (or scariest) part of considering how to connect with them in new ways?

4. Bob states that we find our joy by "helping other people find theirs." What do you think this means? How have you experienced joy through helping others?

5. Is there a difference between joy and happiness? If so, how would you define it?

6. People don't grow where they're *informed*—they grow where they're *accepted*. Where does your small group or church do this well? Where could you all grow?

Respond [15 MINUTES]

(For this activity, you will need a copy of the grid below and a pen or pencil.) During this week's teaching, Bob pointed out that loving your neighbor is something that can start with the people God has put in your world. With this in mind, look at the grid below. This grid represents your neighborhood. The center square with the word "YOU" in it stands for where you live. The empty squares around it represent where your neighbors live.

Take a moment to visualize your neighborhood. Now, see how many of those empty squares you can fill with the actual names of the people who live there. Just do your best. If you live next to the ocean or in the middle of nowhere, just use your office or some other public space where you spend time as your starting place. It's okay. Just fill in as many names as you can.

	YOU	

Look at your grid once it's filled in. What do you notice? Are there any trends? Who do you know well? Who do you not know at all?

Next, circle the neighbor on your grid whom you know the least and with whom you want to make a better connection this week. It might be someone you know a little, and you can invite that person to coffee to get to know them better. Or it could be a person you don't know at all, and your goal for this week is just to learn his or her name. Whatever it is, take a second, say a prayer, and make your plan.

When you're done, share with the group your plan for connecting with a neighbor this week. If anyone in the group is stumped, offer some suggestions. And remember, the goal here is not to convert anyone, or witness, or anything like that. The goal is just to *connect* . . . because that's where it all starts.

Pray [10 MINUTES]

Close the meeting by praying for the specific person you are going to try to meet this week. Pray especially that God would give you the courage to follow through!

 | # Personal Study

Reflect on the content you've covered this week by engaging in the following personal studies. Remember, this part of the study is not about following rules or doing your homework. These activities (categorized as *Do*, *Reflect*, and *Read*) are simply designed to give you the opportunity to jump into loving God and your neighbor with both feet. As you work through each of these exercises, write down your responses to the questions, as you will be given a few minutes to share your insights at the start of the next session. If you are reading *Everybody, Always* alongside this study, first review the prologue and chapters 1–3 of the book.

 | *Do*: Tell Your Story

During this week's teaching, Bob talks about the power of story and how one of the things that happens when you are neighbors with someone is that you get to know each other better and swap stories. This week, you are invited to do this very thing. Pick one or two people from your small group, get together with that person during the week, and just swap stories. You can get together for a meal, a coffee, or just touch base in the church parking lot. Wherever you do it, your goal is simple: *Get to know each other better by sharing a bit of your lives.* Here are a few questions that you can ask to get the stories flowing:

- Where did you grow up?
- How long have you lived where you do now?
- Do you have any siblings? What can you tell me about them?
- Who were and are the most formative people in your life?
- When and how did you get turned on to Jesus and church?
- Why did you decide to participate in this small-group study?
- If you had a whole day to yourself, how would you spend it?
- What is one thing the two of us have in common?

Once you've connected with one of your group members and shared your stories, jot down the following reflections to share next week:

1. How was the experience of sharing stories?

2. Was it easier or harder than you thought? Why?

3. What is something this experience taught you about yourself?

 | *Reflect*: Be Needy

For the Reflect sections of this study guide, you will be reading various passages from the New Testament. This week, read the following teaching of Jesus from Matthew:

> [1] At that time the disciples came to Jesus and asked, "Who, then, is the greatest in the kingdom of heaven?" [2] He called a little child to him, and placed the child among them. [3] And he said: "Truly I tell you, unless you change and become like little children, you will never enter the kingdom of heaven. [4] Therefore, whoever takes the lowly position of this child is the greatest in the kingdom of heaven. [5] And whoever welcomes one such child in my name welcomes me."

MATTHEW 18:1–5

One of the things Jesus is always driving home with his followers is that God's kingdom doesn't work like the kingdoms of this world. God's kingdom is counterintuitive. It has a different set of values. Jesus keeps telling those of us who will listen that we will discover this kingdom in ways we least expect.

This section in the Gospel of Matthew picks up a conversation that Jesus was having with his disciples about this very thing. They had just asked him about who was greatest in his kingdom. Essentially, they wanted to know who was the best in God's new world. They were asking, "Jesus, how do you get to the top of the ladder and succeed in your kingdom?" They wanted to know who would—as Bob puts it in the video—"Get the big chair."

To answer this question, Jesus asked a child to come over to where they were talking. Then he said, "Be like this." Jesus went on to say that unless the disciples changed to become more and more like this child, they wouldn't even figure out how to be part of what God was up to in the world. What was Jesus getting at by saying this to them?

Well, to live in God's world God's way, we have to first let go of all the ways this current world tells us to succeed. The kingdom of God is a place where the "best" are the least and the lowest. It's where the frail and the fragile are powerful. It's a kingdom of downward mobility, and it's a place people often find when they have failed and are in deep need.

This is part of what Jesus was illustrating with the child he called to stand among him and the disciples. Children have needs. They are not self-sufficient. They are dependent and open to help.

It is exactly those qualities that assist us in finding our way into God's new world.

Can you see why a culture that values "pulling yourself up by your bootstraps" might struggle to embrace this message? Success in God's kingdom comes when you stop trying to win and embrace all the ways you keep losing.

1. What else do you think Jesus meant when he talked about becoming like little children?

2. Jesus says "anyone who welcomes a child welcomes me." What does that mean to you?

3. Where are you frustrated by your own need right now?

4. In what ways might this actually be an invitation into the kingdom of God?

 | *Read*: Love People Where You Are

In the Read sections of this study guide, you will have the opportunity to reflect on some of the chapters that you've read in *Everybody, Always*. This week, read the prologue and chapters 1–3 in the book, and then write down your responses to the following questions.

1. Who are some people you know who give away love "like they're made of it"? What are some characteristics you admire in these people?

2. What are some of the barriers you encounter when it comes to loving difficult people? What can you learn from Jesus' example about how to deal with them?

3. What does "extravagant love" look like in your life in terms of "coloring outside the lines" and "going beyond the norms"?

4. Why do you think Jesus asks us to start loving others by first loving our neighbors? Who would you define as being your "neighbors"?

5. What are some ways that you are actively loving your neighbors? How has this involved more than just speaking with them from time to time?

 # Catch Up and Read Ahead

Use this time to go back and complete any of the study and reflection questions from previous studies that you weren't able to finish. Make a note below of any questions you've had and reflect on any growth or personal insights you've gained.

Read chapters 4–6 in *Everybody, Always* before the next group gathering. Use the space below to make note of anything in those chapters that stands out to you or encourages you.

BEFORE GROUP MEETING	Read chapters 4–6 in *Everybody, Always* Read the Welcome section (page 94)
GROUP MEETING	Discuss the Connect questions Read the passage for this session and discuss Watch the video teaching for session 2 Discuss the questions that follow as a group Do the closing exercise and pray (pages 94–98)
STUDY 1: *Do*	Complete the personal study (pages 100–101)
STUDY 2: *Reflect*	Complete the personal study (pages 102–105)
STUDY 3: *Read*	Complete the personal study (page 106)
CATCH UP AND READ AHEAD (BEFORE WEEK 3 GROUP MEETING)	Read chapters 10–12 in *Everybody, Always* Complete any unfinished personal studies (page 107)

Catch People on the Bounce

What I want to do is see the hope
that's inside of people.

BOB GOFF

Welcome [READ ON YOUR OWN]

One of the most popular TED Talks of all time is called "The Power of Vulnerability." It is a talk by Dr. Brené Brown, a research professor who studies empathy and vulnerability.

Dr. Brown has found that empathy and shame are like the opposite ends of an old radio dial. (Remember those?) She says the way a person moves the tuner on the dial toward either empathy or shame is, in fact, all about how vulnerable that person is willing to be.

For instance, if you turn vulnerability all the way up, you will tune in the "empathy station." On this station, through your sharing of experience, you will find connection with another person. However, if you turn vulnerability all the way down, you will end up tuned in to the "shame station," which just shuts everything down.

Possessing the kind of vulnerability that makes empathy happen is difficult, because you have to open yourself up to other people's experiences. You have to be willing to see the world through their eyes and imagine what it's like to stand in their shoes. This costs you something.

However, shame is what happens in the absence of vulnerability. Shame occurs when, because you've been hurt by others in the past, you armor up, vowing, "That's never going to happen to me again!" As a result, shame produces fear, suspicion, and isolation. So, empathy connects you with other people, while shame drives you further apart.

This week, you will be invited to consider these categories of *empathy* and *shame* when it comes to loving the people in your orbit that you might find a "little creepy." Instead of judging them, you will be asked to consider where they've come from and what they've been through. Doing this will keep love flowing, and it will put you in the position where you are open to "catching people on the bounce."

Connect [10 MINUTES]

If you or any of your group members don't know each other, take a few minutes to introduce yourselves. Then discuss the following questions:

- What was your first job? Do you have good memories or bad memories of the experience? Explain.

- What is something that resonated with you in last week's personal study that you would like to share with the group?

Read [10 MINUTES]

Ask someone to read the following passage, and then discuss the questions that follow.

[13] When Jesus came to the region of Caesarea Philippi, he asked his disciples, "Who do people say the Son of Man is?"

[14] They replied, "Some say John the Baptist; others say Elijah; and still others, Jeremiah or one of the prophets."

[15] "But what about you?" he asked. "Who do you say I am?"

[16] Simon Peter answered, "You are the Messiah, the Son of the living God."

[17] Jesus replied, "Blessed are you, Simon son of Jonah, for this was not revealed to you by flesh and blood, but by my Father in heaven. [18] And I tell you that you are Peter, and on this rock I will build my church, and the gates of Hades will not overcome it. [19] I will give you the keys of the kingdom of heaven; whatever you bind on earth will be bound in heaven, and whatever you loose on earth will be loosed in heaven." [20] Then he ordered his disciples not to tell anyone that he was the Messiah.

MATTHEW 16:13–20

When Jesus calls Peter the rock on which he will "build his church," do you think he is rewarding Peter for his answer or naming something about Peter that is already true? Explain.

Why do you think Jesus instructs the disciples not to tell anyone that he is the Messiah?

Watch [20 MINUTES]

Play the video segment for session two. As you watch, use the following outline to record any thoughts or concepts that stand out to you.

Instead of telling people what they want, tell them who they are.

Recognize that God made people just like he made you—and he made you to know others.

The best way you can express your faith to people is to tell them who they are becoming.

God found you right where you are, and you can find other people the same way.

The story of the gospel is that Jesus jumped out of heaven to be with us.

Talk about the right stuff behind people's backs: who they're turning into, not who they used to be.

Don't let shame distance you from God, and don't let it distance you from others.

Follow Jesus to people who are hurting—who have hit the ground hard—and catch them on the bounce.

Discuss [30 MINUTES]

Discuss what you just watched by answering the following questions.

1. In this week's teaching, Bob says we need to stop telling people *what they want* and start telling them *who they are*. What does this mean to you?

2. How do you love difficult people but also have appropriate boundaries with them?

3. What do you think makes it so appealing to say the bad stuff about each other instead of the good stuff?

4. In the video, Bob says that in the end, we're all "turning into love." What questions do you have about that statement? Do you think he is right?

5. Do you agree that showing love "with an agenda" isn't actually showing love toward the people in your world? Why or why not?

6. What does it mean to "catch people on the bounce"? How can doing this give the people in your life a clear view of the hope that Jesus offers to them?

Respond [15 MINUTES]

(For this activity, you will need one 2" x 4" slip of paper, a separate sheet of paper, a pen or pencil, and tape. The group will need one basket or bowl for collecting the papers.)

In the video, Bob stresses how naming what is good and virtuous in others can actually bring those kinds of qualities out of them. So, today, you and your group will give this a try.

Begin by writing your name on one of the 2" x 4" slips of paper. Drop the paper in a basket or bowl and pass it around the group. Then pass the basket around again and take one slip of paper out with another person's name on it. Make sure that if you happen to draw your own name, you put it back in the basket and take a different one.

Next, use the separate piece of paper you have to write a message to the person whose name you drew. Make sure the message includes one or two things you hope for them as well as anything you've noticed about them that's terrific. You can write a generic message if you don't know the person (such as, "I hope you have a great week," "I pray that you sleep really well every night," or, "I hope you will know how much God loves you"). Or it can be a more specific sentiment if you know the person well.

Once everyone in the group is finished, fold the paper with the message in half. Tape the slip of paper with the person's name on it to the front of the folded paper. Now fold *that* over one more time and return the whole thing to the basket. When everyone has turned in their papers to the basket, find the slip with your name on it, and then read the note written to you. Afterward, reflect on these questions:

- How did it feel to read the message?
- Did you find it easier to write the message or to read the message? Why?
- Do you want to share your message with the group?

Invite everyone to remember these messages throughout the week and to really "own" them. They represent *who you are and who you are becoming.*

Pray [10 MINUTES]

Close the meeting by praying for specific individuals in your life whom you know have gone through tough times lately or who are dealing with issues of shame. Ask that God would use you to "catch them on the bounce."

 | # Personal Study

In the group time this week, you were asked to put yourself in the shoes of the people in your world whom you might normally be tempted to judge. In these personal studies, you will continue to explore this idea. As you work through the exercises, be sure to write down your responses, as you will be given time to share at the start of the next session. If you are reading *Everybody, Always* alongside this study, first review chapters 4–6 of the book.

 | # *Do*: Talk About the Right Stuff

In the video teaching for this session, Bob suggested that we "start talking behind each other's backs, but talk about the right stuff. Talk about who people are turning into. Say, 'Have you seen Sally? Have you seen who she's turning into?' Or, 'Seen that pastor? Seen who he's turning into?' Find these beautiful things. Talk it up. Don't make it up."

This week, pick three people in your life who represent rings of familiarity on your tree. Start with someone in your inner ring who is close to you, like a family member or friend. Next, pick someone who is three rings or so out from that place, such as an acquaintance or someone you meet up with on occasion. Finally, pick someone who is four or five rings out from that spot. This could be a person who is distant from you because you don't know him or her well, or because you're critical of the person, or even because he or she is your enemy.

Once you've settled on your three people, write their names in the space provided below. Next, write down three kind, friendly, and complimentary statements you are going to make about them behind their backs. You can say these statements to your coworkers, friends, people at church, or anyone else who is at least familiar with the person. Just make sure that you actually say these things to *someone* in your world during the week.

Person #1: ____

Three statements you will make about this individual:

- ____
- ____
- ____

Person #2: ____

Three statements you will make about this individual:

- ____
- ____
- ____

Person #3: ____

Three statements you will make about this individual:

- ____
- ____
- ____

1. Once you've practiced some good, positive gossip about these individuals, see how it feels. What was it like? Did it change anything about how you saw them?

2. Did this exercise change anything about how you saw yourself? (If so, keep track of your thoughts, make some notes below, and share them next week.)

 | *Reflect*: Stop Keeping Score

In this week's reading, you will be going through one of Jesus' most famous parables, known as the parable of the prodigal son (or two sons). Take a moment to read through this story:

[11] Jesus continued: "There was a man who had two sons. [12] The younger one said to his father, 'Father, give me my share of the estate.' So, he divided his property between them.

[13] "Not long after that, the younger son got together all he had, set off for a distant country and there squandered his wealth in wild living. [14] After he had spent everything, there was a severe famine in that whole country, and he began to be in need. [15] So he went and hired himself out to a citizen of that country, who sent him to his fields to feed pigs. [16] He longed to fill his stomach with the pods that the pigs were eating, but no one gave him anything.

[17] "When he came to his senses, he said, 'How many of my father's hired servants have food to spare, and here I am starving to death! [18] I will set out and go back to my father and say to him: Father, I have sinned against heaven and against you. [19] I am no longer worthy to be called your son; make me like one of your hired servants.' [20] So he got up and went to his father.

"But while he was still a long way off, his father saw him and was filled with compassion for him; he ran to his son, threw his arms around him and kissed him.

[21] "The son said to him, 'Father, I have sinned against heaven and against you. I am no longer worthy to be called your son.'

[22] "But the father said to his servants, 'Quick! Bring the best robe and put it on him. Put a ring on his finger and sandals on his feet. [23] Bring the fattened calf and kill it. Let's have a feast and celebrate. [24] For this son of mine was dead and is alive again; he was lost and is found.' So they began to celebrate.

[25] "Meanwhile, the older son was in the field. When he came near the house, he heard music and dancing. [26] So he called one of the servants and asked him what was going on. [27] 'Your brother has come,' he replied, 'and your father has killed the fattened calf because he has him back safe and sound.'

[28] "The older brother became angry and refused to go in. So his father went out and pleaded with him. [29] But he answered his father, 'Look! All these years I've been slaving for

you and never disobeyed your orders. Yet you never gave me even a young goat so I could celebrate with my friends. ³⁰ But when this son of yours who has squandered your property with prostitutes comes home, you kill the fattened calf for him!'

³¹ "'My son,' the father said, 'you are always with me, and everything I have is yours. ³² But we had to celebrate and be glad, because this brother of yours was dead and is alive again; he was lost and is found.'"

LUKE 15:11–32

One of the brilliant truths hanging around this parable is that in life, you will come across people who just seem to be keeping score. They are the ones who always seem to be writing down all the good they have done and all the wrongs that others have done. In the story, we've got two brothers and a dad. The younger brother basically tells his dad that he wishes he were dead, and then he leaves town with half of the family money. He goes on to waste all that money and eventually winds up in poverty.

Finally, he comes to his senses. He decides to return home to see if he can work for his dad so he can simply eat. But his dad not only welcomes him home but also throws him a huge party to boot. It's an outrageous, even irresponsible, act of mercy.

But there's another brother in the story, and he doesn't like what he sees. This is because the older brother in the parable is a "scorekeeper." He feels that he has been playing by the rules. He has kept his head down and his nose clean. And he cannot stomach the idea of his dad accepting his young brother back . . . much less throwing him a party!

Perhaps you know a scorekeeper or two in your life. These are the friends or family members who seem to be walking around with a ledger, always keeping track of the good they are doing and the bad that everyone else is doing. Then, when an opportune moment arrives, they tally the score and remind you of it. If something bad happened to the person on their ledger, they remind you that he or she "had it coming." Or, if something good happened to the person, they complain that "it's not fair," because they've done so much more good.

But in the parable, Jesus turns the notion of scorekeeping on its head. The God character in the story, the father, is ready to celebrate the return of the younger son just because he loves him. He hasn't been keeping score of the younger son's wrongs. He doesn't make the son work for him to teach him a lesson or even make him take any vows to never stray again. The father seems to think mercy is more valuable.

Furthermore, the father's actions demonstrate a way of seeing the world that isn't limited. Not only does he refuse to keep score, but he also doesn't see the need to divide things up equally in order to "make things fair." He doesn't throw the older son a separate party to reward his actions or even acknowledge all the things the older son has been doing. Why? Because everything the father owns already belongs to the son. For the father, it's a limitless world where there's plenty to go around and nobody has to keep score. It's about grace—and grace is not something we earn by following the rules. It's a gift we simply receive.

This is what Jesus invites us to think about in this parable. Do we see the world like the father, or are we more like the older brother? As the older brother stands with his dad, watching the party begin, will he go inside and join it? Will he let go of his scorecard and rejoice in his father's generosity? Or will he just stay in his tired, old ways?

1. In what ways can you relate to the scorekeeping nature of the older brother?

2. In what ways has God shown you mercy like the father did to the younger brother?

3. How do you respond to the idea that God doesn't feel the need to divide things equally to "keep everything fair"?

4. How does this parable challenge you to change your mindset toward others?

5. Do you think the older brother ever joined the party? More importantly, what would you do if you were in his place?

 | *Read*: Catch People on the Bounce

This week, read through chapters 4–6 in *Everybody, Always*, and then write down your responses to the following questions.

1. Does your Christian practice feel more like *faith* or *compliance* these days? Explain.

2. Is there a relationship where you've let shame create a barrier between you and someone else? If so, what would it look like to heal that divide?

3. What does it mean to build a *kingdom* rather than a *castle* when it comes to accepting others who are different from you?

4. What are some ways to love the difficult people in your life "thirty seconds at a time"?

5. Why is it so important to react to those who have failed with compassion and understanding instead of disapproval or indifference?

Catch Up and Read Ahead

Use this time to go back and complete any of the study and reflection questions from previous studies that you weren't able to finish. Make a note below of any questions you've had and reflect on any growth or personal insights you've gained.

Read chapters 10–12 in *Everybody, Always* before the next group gathering. Use the space below to make note of anything in those chapters that stands out to you or encourages you.

BEFORE GROUP MEETING	Read chapters 10–12 in *Everybody, Always* Read the Welcome section (page 110)
GROUP MEETING	Discuss the Connect questions Read the passage for this session and discuss Watch the video teaching for session 3 Discuss the questions that follow as a group Do the closing exercise and pray (pages 110–114)
STUDY 1: *Do*	Complete the personal study (page 116)
STUDY 2: *Reflect*	Complete the personal study (pages 117–119)
STUDY 3: *Read*	Complete the personal study (page 120)
CATCH UP AND READ AHEAD (BEFORE WEEK 4 GROUP MEETING)	Read chapters 14–16 in *Everybody, Always* Complete any unfinished personal studies (page 121)

Don't Play It Safe

Playing it safe will steal your joy.

BOB GOFF

Welcome [READ ON YOUR OWN]

Jesus really irritated the religious people of his day. They were always getting mad at something he said or did, especially when it came to the poor. One time, some of these folks were questioning Jesus' authority. They thought Jesus didn't have the right to say all the stuff he was saying.

Jesus responded by telling a story (as he often did) and then ended with this statement: "Truly I tell you, the tax collectors and the prostitutes are entering the kingdom of God ahead of you" (Matthew 21:31). As you can imagine, that really got under these religious people's skin! But why would Jesus say this? Tax collectors and prostitutes were the immoral folks nobody liked. They had blown it and nose-dived in their choices in all the ways the moral religious people had not. How could these failures-at-life be plugging into God's world first?

Well, according to Jesus, it was precisely the fact they *had* failed that made the difference. One of the things that gets in the way of us connecting with God is our self-sufficiency. Even if we follow all the rules, do all the right stuff, and pray all the right ways, we can still miss God if we're doing it all by our own strength. This is because we are most open to God when we are needy, busted, and broken. It is in our failures that we most easily find God, not in our great achievements.

This is why Jesus said the prostitutes and tax collectors were entering God's kingdom ahead of the "proper" religious folks. They knew all too well what it was like to be broken and needy. Society didn't work for them, and they had been pushed to the edges and looked down on because of it. However, in the great mystery of the gospel, that marginalization is exactly what opened them up to finding grace. And find it they did! This upside-down dynamic is what this session is all about. It's about getting real enough regarding our own failures to meet the God who wants nothing more than to lavish his grace on us. So, how about it? Are you ready for grace? If so, get ready to get real about it as we jump into this week's teaching.

Connect [10 MINUTES]

Start by discussing the following questions as a group:

- What is something in your life that you've failed at badly? What did you learn from the experience?

- What is something that resonated with you in last week's personal study that you would like to share with the group?

Read [10 MINUTES]

Ask someone to read the following passage, and then discuss the questions that follow.

[1] "Be careful not to practice your righteousness in front of others to be seen by them. If you do, you will have no reward from your Father in heaven. [2] So when you give to the needy, do not announce it with trumpets, as the hypocrites do in the synagogues and on the streets, to be honored by others. Truly I tell you, they have received their reward in full. [3] But when you give to the needy, do not let your left hand know what your right hand is doing, [4] so that your giving may be in secret. Then your Father, who sees what is done in secret, will reward you."

MATTHEW 6:1–4

Why do you think announcing "your righteousness in front of others" is hypocritical?

What kind of reward do you think Jesus is talking about in verse 4?

Watch [20 MINUTES]

Play the video for this session. As you watch, use the following outline to record any thoughts or concepts that stand out to you.

If you overidentify with the mistakes you've made and decide to play it safe, you will miss out on some of the best things God has for you.

Jesus doesn't want you to show off your faith—he wants you to live out your faith.

You're not defined by your biggest failure. And you're not defined by your biggest success.

Find a safe place to have that discussion where you say, "Here's where the recital went really bad, and here's what I did next."

Instead of moving away from those who have failed, move toward them—not to be nice, *but to be Jesus*.

Can you get real enough with Jesus to admit that you're not fixed yet? Can you honestly say, "I need a second touch from God"?

Failure is what God uses to remind you of your tremendous need for him.

If you're willing to catch people on the bounce—to find those who creep you out and engage with them in love—people will see Jesus through you.

Discuss [30 MINUTES]

Discuss what you just watched by answering the following questions.

1. In the teaching, Bob makes the point that Christianity is not like a piano recital: We don't follow Jesus for an audience on stage. Have you ever been tempted to perform your faith for others? If so, when and where?

2. What does it mean to move toward people who have failed and not away from them? How does that work?

3. What's the difference between "being nice" and "being Jesus"?

4. Do you know your blind spots—those areas in which you may not be perceiving the situation accurately? Who is the person in your life who helps you to see them?

5. Have you ever made a mistake that you have had a hard time getting over? What made getting over it so difficult for you?

6. Do you think this group is safe enough for you to get real and say, "I'm not fixed yet"? Why or why not?

Respond [15 MINUTES]

(For this activity, you will need an index card and a pen or pencil.) For the remainder of this session, you and your group will spend time sharing real stuff and getting honest about your mistakes. As Bob said in the teaching, it is at this place that we meet God and community happens. Start by grabbing an index card and a pen or pencil.

On the index card, write down a mistake you have made that you fear you might be "overidentifying" with. These are the kinds of mistakes that can keep you from jumping toward the life that God has for you—the ones that make you want to stop trying and play it safe by never putting yourself out there again. Be honest. No one is going to read the card but you.

Once everyone in the group has written something down, take the index card you've written and ball it up in your hand. Stand with the group in a circle, and then take two steps back (to make sure everybody has some space). Once everyone is in position, reflect on the trouble this mistake has caused you and the way you realize it has held you. Next, consider if you would like for things to be different.

As everyone in the group is thinking about this, take a jump forward as a way of saying yes to God's invitation of a new life! The jump doesn't have to be big (actually, it shouldn't be—be careful!), and it can also be a step forward if you can't jump or don't have room. Likewise, if you're seated and can't stand, feel free to move a foot or finger forward.

Basically, whatever action you take, make it symbolize your desire to jump toward the new life God has for you and stop playing it safe.

Pray [10 MINUTES]

As you and the group members stand together in the circle, close by having one person read the words of Psalm 23:1–4 as a prayer and promise from God: *"The LORD is my shepherd, I lack nothing. He makes me lie down in green pastures, he leads me beside quiet waters, he refreshes my soul. He guides me along the right paths for his name's sake. Even though I walk through the darkest valley, I will fear no evil, for you are with me."* Say "amen" together and call it a night!

 # Personal Study

In this week's group time, you reflected on the importance of getting real about your failures and allowing God to lavish his grace on you. In this week's personal study, you will continue to explore these ideas. As you work through the exercises, continue to write down your responses, as you will be given time to share at the start of the next session. If you are reading *Everybody, Always* alongside this study, first review chapters 10–12 of the book.

 | *Do*: Move Toward Others

During the teaching, Bob said, "Instead of moving away from [broken, needy, and creepy people], our idea is to move toward them. Not just to be nice, but to be Jesus." For this week's *Do* activity, you are invited to take a risk . . . and literally move toward folks who are vulnerable and needy.

Identify a place where there are people for whom the systems of our society are not working. This might be a public park, a rescue shelter, a bus station, or anywhere else people who are intimately acquainted with struggle and even failure might be hanging out. Once you're in this space, just sit and be present for at least thirty minutes.

As you are doing this, pray and ask God to show you where he is present—and also evaluate your own discomfort. What are you learning about yourself in this place? What are you learning about these people's struggles? Most importantly, what are you learning about God?

Reflect on your experience, make some notes below, and share with the other group members next week.

1. What did you learn about yourself through this activity?

2. What did you learn about the struggles of the people in that place?

3. What did you learn about God as a result?

This week's reading centers around a discussion that Jesus had with his disciples after they passed a man on the road who had been blind since birth:

[1] As he went along, he saw a man blind from birth. [2] His disciples asked him, "Rabbi, who sinned, this man or his parents, that he was born blind?"

[3] "Neither this man nor his parents sinned," said Jesus, "but this happened so that the works of God might be displayed in him. [4] As long as it is day, we must do the works of him who sent me. Night is coming, when no one can work. [5] While I am in the world, I am the light of the world."

[6] After saying this, he spit on the ground, made some mud with the saliva, and put it on the man's eyes. [7] "Go," he told him, "wash in the Pool of Siloam" (this word means "Sent"). So the man went and washed, and came home seeing.

[8] His neighbors and those who had formerly seen him begging asked, "Isn't this the same man who used to sit and beg?" [9] Some claimed that he was.

Others said, "No, he only looks like him."

But he himself insisted, "I am the man."

[10] "How then were your eyes opened?" they asked.

[11] He replied, "The man they call Jesus made some mud and put it on my eyes. He told me to go to Siloam and wash. So I went and washed, and then I could see."

JOHN 9:1–11

One of the things we tend to do when things go wrong is find someone to blame. Whether it's little things or big things, blaming someone else for our troubles is pretty common. People have done it for thousands of years . . . and it's not going away anytime soon. But here's the thing about blaming: *Jesus isn't interested in it.*

In the story above, Jesus runs into a man who has been blind his whole life. Immediately, his disciples ask whose fault it is. Now, this was a common question in Jesus' day. Everyone agreed that a physical disability was someone's fault—they just disagreed as to whose fault it was. So, the disciples are genuinely curious. *Was this guy's blindness a result of something he did? Or something his mom and dad did?*

They are asking Jesus to put the whole matter to rest. However, as Jesus so often does, he transcends the circumstance by inviting the disciples to see how God is working at a whole other level. Jesus explains the man's blindness was neither his nor his parents' fault. Instead, he says, "This happened so that the works of God might be displayed in him."

Then Jesus heals him. *Boom.* He wasn't interested in who was at fault in this man's situation. He knew the disciples were asking the wrong question. And he was attentive to what God was going to do next. This is where it gets interesting for us as well.

When things have gone wrong in our lives, we can spend a ton of time dwelling on whose fault it was and resent the people whom we feel got us into this spot. And, to be fair, sometimes we need to do this. Forgiveness and reconciliation can only happen when we name and acknowledge the truths about what has happened to us. However, we can't stay there.

Healing involves moving forward and looking to see what God is going to do next. Our God is a God who wastes nothing. There is no event so sad and broken that he can't bring something new and beautiful out of it. It is what God does, and that's a good thing. The question is whether *we can trust what God is doing.* Can we bring the broken events in our lives to God and trust him to make something beautiful out of them?

Jesus says this is what God does. The question is, do you believe it?

1. How do you respond to this scene in John 9:1–11? In what ways have you seen people today asking the same question as the disciples?

2. Where are you feeling the most tempted to look backward and assign blame for the hard things in your life?

3. When was a time when something good emerged out of a sad and tragic circumstance?

4. Do you think this kind of thing could happen for you again? Why or why not?

 | *Read*: Don't Play It Safe

This week, read through chapters 10–12 in *Everybody, Always*, and then write down your responses to the following questions.

1. Why is it important to not always be looking for the "green lights" when it comes to boldly stepping out in faith and loving others?

2. How have you witnessed Jesus helping you to "see more" spiritually as you've continued to follow him?

3. When has a voice of defeat tempted you to quit what you knew God was leading you to do? How did you respond to that situation?

4. When you think about the word *evangelism*, does it bring up positive or negative associations? Why did you answer the way you did?

5. Jesus invites us to move from merely identifying with someone's pain to standing with that person in it. What is the difference between the two? Where is a place in your life that you have an opportunity to stand in someone's pain with him or her?

Catch Up and Read Ahead

Use this time to go back and complete any of the study and reflection questions from previous studies that you weren't able to finish. Make a note below of any questions you've had and reflect on any growth or personal insights you've gained.

Read chapters 14–16 in *Everybody, Always* before the next group gathering. Use the space below to make note of anything in those chapters that stands out to you or encourages you.

BEFORE GROUP MEETING	Read chapters 14–16 in *Everybody, Always* Read the Welcome section (page 124)
GROUP MEETING	Discuss the Connect questions Read the passage for this session and discuss Watch the video teaching for session 4 Discuss the questions that follow as a group Do the closing exercise and pray (pages 124–128)
STUDY 1: *Do*	Complete the personal study (page 130)
STUDY 2: *Reflect*	Complete the personal study (pages 131–133)
STUDY 3: *Read*	Complete the personal study (page 134)
CATCH UP AND READ AHEAD (BEFORE WEEK 5 GROUP MEETING)	Read chapters 20–24 in *Everybody, Always* Complete any unfinished personal studies (page 135)

Look at What's in Your Bucket

I want to have that new car smell, that new creation smell, and I think you do too.

BOB GOFF

Welcome [READ ON YOUR OWN]

In Jesus' day, eating with people was a big deal. This is because if you ate with someone, it meant you were interested in being friends. It meant you accepted that person—and it was a sign to everyone else in the community about what mattered to you.

Based on this, you'd think that Jesus would have picked all the morally upright, virtuous people to eat with. After all, these were the folks who had been "getting it right" and showing everybody else how it was done. It only makes sense that Jesus would want to point them out by having lunch, right? Well, you'd be surprised. Or maybe you wouldn't.

Instead of always eating with the rule-following religious people, Jesus frequently ate with the wrong kinds of people. The people who had blown it. The people who were not respected. The people who were seen as the worst examples of godly living. And here's the thing . . . it drove the religious people nuts.

One time, when some of these religious folks asked Jesus about why he did this, he replied, "It is not the healthy who need a doctor, but the sick. I have not come to call the righteous, but sinners to repentance" (Luke 5:31–32).

Jesus knew that what opens people up to an authentic relationship with God is their need. If this sounds familiar (as in, didn't the last session open with the same lesson?), you'd be right. It is a major theme in Jesus' ministry. But here's where this lesson diverges from the last one: Opening up to God is not just about recognizing your own need but also about moving toward other needy people. Even the ones you may find a bit creepy.

Here's the thing: If you hang around needy people, you'll find Jesus. No doubt. So the question for this week is, "Do you want to meet Jesus?" This session shows how it works.

Connect [10 MINUTES]

Start by discussing the following questions as a group:

- Who was your best friend growing up? Are you still in touch? If not, why do you think the two of you drifted apart?

- What is something that resonated with you in last week's personal study that you would like to share with the group?

Read [10 MINUTES]

Ask someone to read the following passage, and then discuss the questions that follow.

[20] "My prayer is not for them alone. I pray also for those who will believe in me through their message, [21] that all of them may be one, Father, just as you are in me and I am in you. May they also be in us so that the world may believe that you have sent me. [22] I have given them the glory that you gave me, that they may be one as we are one—[23] I in them and you in me—so that they may be brought to complete unity. Then the world will know that you sent me and have loved them even as you have loved me."

JOHN 17:20–23

What do you think Jesus has in mind when he prays that all his disciples would be "one"?

Jesus says the unity of his disciples is what will tell the world that he was sent from God (see verse 23). Is the church today known for its unity? If so, where do you see it? If not, why not?

Watch [20 MINUTES]

Play the video for this session. As you watch, use the following outline to record any thoughts or concepts that stand out to you.

You will turn into whatever you fill your "bucket" with. If you fill it with a bunch of love, you'll turn into love.

The promise of Scripture is that we each get to be new creations.

If you want more faith, do more stuff—and don't do it because Jesus "needs your help." He doesn't need your help, but he does want your heart.

In John 17, Jesus basically said, "If you want to know what it's like between me and my Dad, just see how people are one—and you can't be one if you aren't engaged."

God grows us up by letting us do things and experience uncomfortable things—because comfortable people don't need Jesus. Desperate people do.

Don't just agree with Jesus. Actually do what he says.

Jesus was always available. He had time for *everybody*.

Who is somebody you could engage with whom you've been avoiding? Who is somebody who has kind of creeped you out in the past that you could engage with?

Discuss [30 MINUTES]

Discuss what you just watched by answering the following questions.

1. Are there any difficult people or hard circumstances that have grown your faith? If so, who or what were they? How did you grow from them?

2. How would you describe the difference between *agreeing* with Jesus and *doing* what Jesus says? What does this look like in your life?

3. If it is true that you will become whatever you fill your bucket with, then what would you most like to fill your bucket with?

4. Is there anything that you need to take *out* of your bucket in order to live the life God has for you? If so, how will you start to do this?

5. We become open to Jesus when we are uncomfortable, afraid, or in need. What would your next uncomfortable step be in order to be open to God in a new way?

Respond [15 MINUTES]

(For this activity, you will need five to six slips of paper—nothing larger than 1" x 6"—a Styrofoam coffee cup or Dixie cup, and a pen or pencil.)

During the teaching this week, Bob talks about buckets and says that whatever you fill your bucket with, that is what you'll become. Fill it with business deals, and you'll become a business person. Fill it with arguments, and you'll become a lawyer. Fill it with love, and you'll become love. You can fill your bucket with all sorts of good stuff that will help you love others, or you can fill it with all sorts of negative stuff that will get in your way.

So, to close out this time, evaluate what's in your bucket. Start by picking up a pen or pencil and one of the cups. The cup represents your "bucket." Next, using the slips of paper provided, write down a few things in your bucket that get in the way of you doing the stuff Jesus is calling you to do. This could be anything from fear to resentments, work, social media, and the like. Just say a prayer, be honest, and write each one down on a separate slip of paper.

Once you're done, stack your slips of paper face down and set them aside. Remember, no one is going to see this but you. Next, write down two to three things that you want to fill your bucket with. These are the things you want to turn into—the stuff that needs to happen in your life to make reaching out to even the creepiest people possible. Once you're done, stack your slips of paper face down and set them aside. Again, no one should see these but you.

Now, once everyone has their two piles, ball up the slips with the negative stuff written on them and one by one put them into your cup. This is a way of recognizing what is going on in your life now. Say a prayer and take each slip out of your bucket, one at a time. This is a way of saying to God, "I don't want this influence in my life anymore, and I'm ready to get rid of it."

After this—staying in that same place of prayer—take the slips of paper that name what you want to fill your bucket with. Again, one at a time, fold them over and place them in your bucket. As each one goes in, let your prayer be one that says, "God, I need more of this in my life. Please help me make that possible."

But you're not done just yet . . . the surprise twist is that you're going to take your "bucket" with you *everywhere you go this week*. Let it be a symbol of what you're asking God to do in you and a reminder of the kind of person you want to become! Pay attention to how its presence shapes your attitudes and imagination, and pay attention to how God uses it to show you things about him. Take some notes about how it went to share with the group next week.

Pray [10 MINUTES]

Close the meeting by praying that God would help you fill your bucket with the right things. Ask that he would fill your life with his plans so you can become more like him.

 | Personal Study

In this week's group time, you considered the truth that opening up to God is not just about recognizing your *own* need but also about moving toward *other* needy people. You will keep delving into this idea in this week's personal study. As you work through these exercises, keep recording your responses, reflections, take-aways, and breakthroughs, as you will be given time to share at the start of the next session. If you are reading *Everybody, Always* alongside this study, first review chapters 14–16 of the book.

 | *Do*: Be Available

During the video teaching for this week, Bob notes how he does not send anyone to voicemail. He says, "People don't follow vision; they follow availability. And there's something beautiful that happens. Every time I pick up the phone and say 'hello,' I've just answered every question anybody has. People just want to know, 'Is it really true?' They want to know that about you, and they want to know that about me, and we can answer that by saying, 'hello.'"

For this activity, simply spend the rest of the week picking up your phone every time it rings. This might seem crazy, but see what God does with it. And if that's too much trouble, then at least try it for a day or even an afternoon. Just take one step toward being available, and see how Jesus meets you there.

Oh . . . and if you are one of those rare people in the world today who doesn't carry a phone with them wherever they go, it doesn't mean you get out of this. Do other things to be available, like work with the door open in your office, or eat in the break room, or go where people are asking for money on the street and get into a conversation with them. Whatever you choose to do, make note of it below and bring your experiences to share with the group at the next session—and don't forget to take your bucket along.

 | *Reflect*: Now You're Talking

This week's reading is from a story Jesus told that is often called the Parable of the Sheep and the Goats. Take a moment to read through this teaching:

31 "When the Son of Man comes in his glory, and all the angels with him, he will sit on his glorious throne. 32 All the nations will be gathered before him, and he will separate the people one from another as a shepherd separates the sheep from the goats. 33 He will put the sheep on his right and the goats on his left.

34 "Then the King will say to those on his right, 'Come, you who are blessed by my Father; take your inheritance, the kingdom prepared for you since the creation of the world. 35 For I was hungry and you gave me something to eat, I was thirsty and you gave me something to drink, I was a stranger and you invited me in, 36 I needed clothes and you clothed me, I was sick and you looked after me, I was in prison and you came to visit me.'

37 "Then the righteous will answer him, 'Lord, when did we see you hungry and feed you, or thirsty and give you something to drink? 38 When did we see you a stranger and invite you in, or needing clothes and clothe you? 39 When did we see you sick or in prison and go to visit you?'

40 "The King will reply, 'Truly I tell you, whatever you did for one of the least of these brothers and sisters of mine, you did for me.'

41 "Then he will say to those on his left, 'Depart from me, you who are cursed, into the eternal fire prepared for the devil and his angels. 42 For I was hungry and you gave me nothing to eat, I was thirsty and you gave me nothing to drink, 43 I was a stranger and you did not invite me in, I needed clothes and you did not clothe me, I was sick and in prison and you did not look after me.'

44 "They also will answer, 'Lord, when did we see you hungry or thirsty or a stranger or needing clothes or sick or in prison, and did not help you?'

45 "He will reply, 'Truly I tell you, whatever you did not do for one of the least of these, you did not do for me.'

46 "Then they will go away to eternal punishment, but the righteous to eternal life."

MATTHEW 25:31–46

This particular passage from Matthew's Gospel is perhaps one of the most complex and confusing texts in the whole Bible. It is one of those passages that most of us would prefer to just gloss over because, if we're honest, it kind of makes Jesus look bad. There's sheep and goats, great separations, but also . . . eternal punishment. What is going on here?

The answer is lots of things, but for this study we want to look at one particular part of the parable: the big list of stuff that Jesus proclaims, when done to others, is like doing to him. You see the list: feeding the hungry, giving the thirsty a drink, welcoming strangers, clothing the naked, caring for the sick, and visiting people in prison. In the parable, Jesus says the criteria of who ends up a sheep or a goat has to do with these items.

And yet . . . if we have a gospel that is all about grace, unconditional love, and unearned mercy, then doing the right things can't be a way to earn a spot in God's kingdom. If so, it would be the opposite of everything that Jesus had taught up until this point. So, if the lists aren't about that, what are they about?

A while ago, a pastor named Gary Chapman published a book called *The Five Love Languages*. In the book, he talks about how people give and receive love in one of five different ways: (1) acts of service, (2) words of affirmation, (3) quality time, (4) physical touch, and (5) giving gifts. Each of these acts is like a language we use to communicate to others. Using someone's love language is a tangible way to say, "I really care about you."

Is it possible that all these good works Jesus mentions in Matthew 25:31–46—the ones that are on the list—are simply God's *love language*? Might it be the case that the list is not a bunch of things we have to do to try to earn God's love but instead are a description of how to live in ways that say to God, "I really care about you"? As Bob noted, Jesus doesn't want our help, but he does want our heart. Maybe this is just the way to give it to him.

1. What questions does the parable you just read bring up for you?

2. What are some of the ways people show love to you? What is your primary love language to express care to others?

3. If God's love language involves reaching out to people in all kinds of need, where are you already engaged in that kind of service?

4. Are there other opportunities for connecting with the needy that God might be calling you to do as well? If so, what are they?

This week, read through chapters 14–16 in Everybody, Always, and then write down your responses to the following questions.

1. When are a few times that you've seen God leading you from the safest route to the one that helped you grow the most?

2. How would it change your life if you viewed every person you met as Jesus?

3. What is Jesus' ultimate plan for us when it comes to serving others?

4. What do you think Jesus meant when he said that if we make a big deal about what we're doing now—hoping someone will clap—we've already gotten our reward?

5. What has helping others taught you personally about the cost of grace?

Catch Up and Read Ahead

Use this time to go back and complete any of the study and reflection questions from previous studies that you weren't able to finish. Make a note below of any questions you've had and reflect on any growth or personal insights you've gained.

Read chapters 20–24 in *Everybody, Always* before the next group gathering. Use the space below to make note of anything in those chapters that stands out to you or encourages you.

BEFORE GROUP MEETING	Read chapters 20–24 in *Everybody, Always* Read the Welcome section (page 138)
GROUP MEETING	Discuss the Connect questions Read the passage for this session and discuss Watch the video teaching for session 5 Discuss the questions that follow as a group Do the closing exercise and pray (pages 138–142)
STUDY 1: *Do*	Complete the personal study (page 144)
STUDY 2: *Reflect*	Complete the personal study (pages 145–146)
STUDY 3: *Read*	Complete the personal study (page 147)
WRAP IT UP	Connect with someone in your group (page 148) Complete any unfinished personal studies Connect with your group about the next study that you want to go through together

Love Even the Difficult People

God didn't say it would be easy.
He just said it would work.

BOB GOFF

Welcome [READ ON YOUR OWN]

So, what does this all mean for us? This is the big question we're asking in this final session. During the last four sessions, we've discussed how loving Jesus doesn't mean we have to cross the ocean, we just have to cross the street. We've seen that the people who creep us out the most are also our neighbors—and loving them means learning their stories. We've learned that doing this kind of thing can be risky but that, in Jesus, we can become people who take the risk.

All this means there's yet one more step for us to take: *We have to actually do it.* There's a difference between learning about how to do something and actually taking a step to do it. The plan for this final session is to get you thinking about how you are going to love everybody, always. As we will see, this includes your friends, family, and acquaintances, but it also includes the difficult people you don't normally get along with—who might be called your "enemies."

You've been training for this. All the in-between sessions activities have been designed to grow your imagination and stretch your comfort zone so you can make your own plan for what comes next. So take a deep breath, say a prayer, and jump into this session.

And don't worry. If you blow it a time or two, remember that God will always be there to catch you on the bounce.

Connect [10 MINUTES]

Start by discussing the following questions as a group:

- How do you respond to this idea of taking steps to love the difficult people in your life? What are some challenges you might have in doing this?

- What is something that resonated with you in last week's personal study that you would like to share with the group?

Read [10 MINUTES]

Ask someone to read the following passage, and then discuss the questions that follow.

[27] "But to you who are listening I say: Love your enemies, do good to those who hate you, [28] bless those who curse you, pray for those who mistreat you. [29] If someone slaps you on one

cheek, turn to them the other also. If someone takes your coat, do not withhold your shirt from them. [30] Give to everyone who asks you, and if anyone takes what belongs to you, do not demand it back [31] Do to others as you would have them do to you.

[32] "If you love those who love you, what credit is that to you? Even sinners love those who love them. [33] And if you do good to those who are good to you, what credit is that to you? Even sinners do that. [34] And if you lend to those from whom you expect repayment, what credit is that to you? Even sinners lend to sinners, expecting to be repaid in full. [35] But love your enemies, do good to them, and lend to them without expecting to get anything back. Then your reward will be great, and you will be children of the Most High, because he is kind to the ungrateful and wicked. [36] Be merciful, just as your Father is merciful."

LUKE 6:27–36

What is one practical way you've seen someone love his or her enemy?

What does it mean in your life to be merciful just as God is merciful?

Watch [20 MINUTES]

Play the video for this session. As you watch, use the following outline to record any thoughts or concepts that stand out to you.

Your stories, and the way you apply what you've learned about faith to what you've learned in your life, actually have the ability to change people.

If you really want a grade on where you're at in your faith, see how you're treating the people who creep you out.

People who put wheels on their faith are willing to take tremendous risks to do that. Not so they're the hero, or the victim, but so they're a participant.

We don't need to understand everything about forgiveness to get a little of it.

On your very worst day—on that day of your biggest mess-up that you don't want to let anybody know about—God still calls you his *beloved*.

Do you want to be "perfect" bad enough that you're willing to get past all the stuff that is keeping you wrapped around the axle?

Instead of trying to figure everybody out, just love everybody.

What's your next step to move a little closer to the Author of love? What is your next step to move toward loving everybody, always?

Discuss [30 MINUTES]

Discuss what you just watched by answering the following questions.

1. Consider Bob's story in this week's teaching about Kabi the witch doctor. What stuck out to you, touched you, or even inspired you?

2. Do you relate to Bob's statement about spending his whole life avoiding the very people Jesus was always engaging? Why or why not?

3. Have you ever been someone else's enemy? Do you know why?

4. Is it easier for you to forgive others or to receive forgiveness from others? Why might this be the case?

5. What are some healthy precautions to take in dealing with those people who are just unsafe to be around? How can these precautions keep you from being stuck in fear when it comes to approaching them?

6. What is the most threatening part of Bob's challenge to "just do it" when it comes to loving your enemies?

Respond [15 MINUTES]

(For this activity, you will need one sheet of paper and a pen or pencil.) For the past four weeks, you've engaged in this study through group discussion and activities designed to help you learn to love everybody, always. These activities have been provided for you. But this week, it's your turn.

On the sheet of paper, make a list of your "enemies." Now, these can be *actual* enemies, meaning people who are actively trying to do you harm. They can also be the people you have avoided in the past—including somebody from whom you're estranged, or even somebody from whom you've kept your distance because he or she wounded you deeply.

Once you and your group members have completed the list, take five minutes to write beside each name several ways you can connect with that person. This could be via social media, through email, by a text, or through a common acquaintance—anything will do for a starting point. Next, pick one person on the list who you will reach out to and love after the study is over. Sketch out your plan on the paper for how you're actually going to do it.

After the five minutes are up, share with the group some of what you've written. Tell them the person on the list whom you are going to approach. Remember, if any of the people on your list are dangerous or unsafe, be smart about all this and ask the group for advice and guidance. The idea is to leave this session with a plan for what your next step toward loving others will be.

Use the following questions to reflect on the experience of the study as a whole.

Before going through this study, I used to think ____

____,

but now I wonder ____

____.

The best thing about this experience was ____

____.

The worst thing was ____

____.

If I could describe my *Everybody, Always* experience in one word, it would be: ______________

____.

Pray [10 MINUTES]

Close the meeting by praying that God would give you the courage to not just *agree* with Jesus but actually go out and *do* what he says. Then pray that God would help you to not allow fear to hold you back in truly loving everybody, always.

 | # Personal Study

Congratulations! You've taken up the challenge to love everybody, always and have now completed the study. In this final session, you've also taken the big step of considering what you need to do next to put all of what you've learned into practice. This last personal study will continue to help you think through practical ways to do this. As you work through each of these exercises, continue to journal your responses. If you are reading *Everybody, Always* alongside this study, first review chapters 20–24 of the book.

 | *Do*: Bless Your Heart

The challenge for today is to follow up on the next step you formulated with your group. This is part of the grand adventure you are invited to join when you follow Jesus! Don't pay your discipleship as lip service only. Get out there this week and take that next step! But, if you're stuck and don't know how to move toward this goal, here's a place to start.

In the book of Romans, Paul says you should "bless those who persecute you; bless and do not curse" (12:14). One way to live out this teaching is to call to mind one of the enemies you listed during the group time—the one you find it the hardest of all to love. Then, while you're holding that person in your thoughts, ask that God would bless him or her.

That's it. It's that simple. Except that when you try it, you will probably find that it's not! Offering a prayer of blessing for someone who has hurt you or done wrong to you can feel really weird. But that's because God is using it to grow you and set you free.

Now, keep in mind that you are not blessing the person so he or she has some sort of divine encounter with God (though that would be cool, wouldn't it?). Rather, you are blessing that person so *you* can be released from the stuff that clogs your heart—things like hate, bitterness, and resentment. You are blessing that person because it's good for both of you and, on the off chance that the opportunity arises for you to reconcile, you will be ready.

So, go forth and bless that person's heart . . . in the name of Jesus. After you have done this, take a few minutes to reflect on what the experience meant for you.

Read the following passage from Paul's letter to the church in Corinth:

[5] If anyone has caused grief, he has not so much grieved me as he has grieved all of you to some extent—not to put it too severely. [6] The punishment inflicted on him by the majority is sufficient. [7] Now instead, you ought to forgive and comfort him, so that he will not be overwhelmed by excessive sorrow. [8] I urge you, therefore, to reaffirm your love for him. [9] Another reason I wrote you was to see if you would stand the test and be obedient in everything. [10] Anyone you forgive, I also forgive. And what I have forgiven—if there was anything to forgive—I have forgiven in the sight of Christ for your sake, [11] in order that Satan might not outwit us. For we are not unaware of his schemes.

2 CORINTHIANS 2:5–11

Paul has been corresponding with these believers, and it appears that one of their members did something inappropriate to him. We don't know what it was, but we do know that Paul is aware of it and has heard how the community worked through it with the person. As a result, even though Paul hasn't yet reconciled with the offender, he tells the church the way they forgave the person is all he needs. As of now, he's good. The Corinthians don't need to protect his honor by shaming this guy anymore. Their witness of forgiveness is all he needs.

Could there be a more different attitude from what we find today? Holding grudges is like an Olympic sport in our culture. Oftentimes, we're not even holding grudges against the people who did anything to us—we're holding them against people who did stuff to our friends, spouses, or kids. The problem is that this is not helping. In fact, it's making us sick, because it's forcing us to store up all sorts of resentment and pain in our hearts. We think we're holding the grudge to punish the other person when in fact we're just hurting ourselves.

So, today, follow the example of Paul. If there is somebody who is hard for you to love, don't let a mistake that person made with someone else be a roadblock for you. Instead, choose to forgive that person.

1. What strikes you about Paul's words to the church in 2 Corinthians 2:5–11?

2. Are you currently carrying a grudge about something that happened to a loved one? If so, what is it?

3. What would need to happen for you to be able to forgive the offender and let it go?

4. What would you need from God to make that possible?

Read: Love Even the Difficult People

This week, read chapters 20–24 in *Everybody, Always,* and then write down your responses to the following questions.

1. What are some situations you are facing right now where you need to hear God say, "Be not afraid"? What would it take for you to be courageous in that situation?

2. When are some times that God blew your mind and used unbelievable things to help you experience his power?

3. Each day, we get to decide whether we're really following Jesus or treating him like "he's just a Sherpa carrying our stuff." What is the difference between the two?

4. When you think about your life, do you tend to look at how far you have to go or see how far you have come? Why do you think you answered like you did?

5. How have you seen your life change as you've learned to love difficult people? How have you seen your loving actions change another person's life? Explain your response.

Wrap It Up

Use this time to go back and complete any of the study and reflection questions from previous days that you weren't able to finish. Make note of what God has revealed to you in these days. Finally, talk with your group about what study you may want to go through next. Put a date on the calendar for when you'll meet next to study God's Word and dive deeper into community.

Leader's Guide

T hank you for giving of your time and talents to lead your group though *Love Does* and/or *Everybody, Always*. What you have chosen to do is important, and good fruit can come from studies like these. The rewards of being a leader are different from those of participating, and we hope that you will find your own walk with Jesus deepened by this experience.

Love Does and *Everybody, Always* are five-session studies built around video content and small-group interaction. As the group leader, imagine yourself as the host of a party. Your job is to take care of your guests by managing all the behind-the-scenes details so that as your guests arrive, they can focus on each other and on interaction around the topic.

As the group leader, your role is not to answer all the questions or reteach the content—the video, book, and study guide will do most of that work. Your job is to guide the experience and cultivate your small group into a kind of teaching community. This will make it a place for members to process, question, and reflect—not necessarily receive more instruction.

There are several elements in this leader's guide that will help you as you structure your study time, so be sure to follow along and take advantage of each one.

Before You Begin

Before your first meeting, make sure the group members have a copy of this study guide so they can follow along and have their answers written out ahead of time. This will keep everyone on the same page and help the process run smoothly. Alternatively, you can hand out the study guides at your first meeting and give the members time to look over the material and ask any preliminary questions. Be sure they are aware that they have access to the streaming videos at any time by following the instructions provided with this guide.

Encourage each participant (or couple) to also get a copy of the books that accompany these studies. This is so they can complete the Reflect portion of the personal studies each week. If this is not possible, you might want to check to see if your church or anyone from the group is willing to donate an extra copy or two for sharing. During your first meeting, send a sheet of paper around the room and have the members write down their names, phone numbers, and email addresses so you can keep in touch with them during the week.

Generally, the ideal size for a group is about eight to ten people, which will ensure that everyone has enough time to participate in discussions. If you have more people, break up the main group into smaller subgroups. Encourage those who show up at the first meeting to commit to attending the duration of the study, as this will help the group members get to know each other, create stability for the group, and help you know how to prepare each week.

Hospitality

You will want to create an environment conducive to sharing and learning. For this reason, a church sanctuary or formal classroom may not be as ideal for your weekly meetings, as they can feel formal and less intimate. Whatever venue you choose, make sure there is enough comfortable seating for everyone in the group and, if possible, arrange the seats in a semicircle so everyone can see the video easily. This will make the transition between the video and group conversation more efficient and natural.

Try to get to the meeting site early so you can greet the participants as they arrive. Simple refreshments create a welcoming atmosphere and can be a wonderful addition to a group study evening. If you do serve food, take into account any food allergies or dietary restrictions your group may have. Also, if you meet in a home, you will want to find out if the house has pets (in case there are any allergies) and even consider offering childcare to couples with children who want to attend.

Finally, be sure your media technology is working properly. Managing these details up front will make the rest of your group experience flow more smoothly and provide a welcoming space in which to engage the content of both *Love Does* and *Everybody, Always*.

Structuring the Discussion Time

You will need to determine how long you want your meetings to last so that you can plan your time accordingly. Suggested times for each section have been provided in this guide, and if you adhere to these times, your group will meet for ninety minutes. However, many groups like to meet for two hours. If this describes your particular group, follow the times listed in the right-hand column of the chart given below.

SECTION	90 MINUTES	120 MINUTES
CONNECT (discuss one or more of the opening questions for the session)	10 minutes	15 minutes
READ (read the opening passage and discuss together as a group)	10 minutes	15 minutes
WATCH (watch the teaching material together and take notes)	10–20 minutes	10–20 minutes
DISCUSS (discuss the study questions you selected ahead of time)	30–35 minutes	40–50 minutes
RESPOND (do the closing activity on your own and write down key takeaways)	15–20 minutes	20 minutes
PRAY (pray together and dismiss)	10 minutes	10 minutes

As the group leader, it is up to you to keep track of the time and keep things moving along according to your schedule. You might want to set a timer for each segment so both you and the group members know when your time is up. (There are some good phone apps for timers that play a gentle chime or other pleasant sound instead of a disruptive noise.)

Leading Your Group

If you are new to leading a small group, what follows are some simple tips for making your group time healthy, enjoyable, and effective. First, consider beginning the meeting with a word of prayer. Then remind people to silence and put away their mobile phones. This is a way to say "yes" to being present to one another and to God.

Each session begins with an opening reflection in the Welcome section. The questions that follow in the Connect section serve as icebreakers to get the group members thinking about the topic at hand. Some people may want to tell a long story in response to one of these questions, but the goal is to keep the answers brief. Ideally, you want everyone in the group to get a chance to answer, so try to keep the responses to a minute or less. If you have talkative group members, say up front that everyone needs to limit the answer to one minute.

Give the group members a chance to answer, but tell them to feel free to pass if they wish. With the rest of the study, it's generally not a good idea to have everyone answer every question—a free-flowing discussion is more desirable. But with the opening icebreaker questions, you can go around the circle. Encourage shy people to share, but don't force them.

After this checking-in time, your group will engage in a short Bible study (in the Read section) that will lead into the video teaching. You do not need to be a biblical scholar to lead this effectively! Your role is simply to open up conversation by using the instructions provided and inviting the group into the biblical text. Following this, the group will watch Bob on the video and then answer some small-group discussion questions. As the discussion progresses, use comments such as, "Tell me more about that," or, "Why did you answer the way you did?" This invites meaningful sharing from the participants in a nonthreatening way.

Note that you have been given multiple questions to use in each session. You do not have to use them all or follow them in order. Feel free to pick and choose questions based on either the needs of your group or how the conversation is flowing. Also, don't be afraid of silence. Offering a question and allowing up to thirty seconds of "nothingness" is okay. It allows people space to think about how they want to respond and gives them time to do so.

As the group leader, you are the boundary keeper for your group. Do not let anyone (yourself included) dominate the group time. Keep an eye out for group members who might be tempted to attack folks they disagree with or try and "fix" those having struggles. These kind of behaviors can derail a group's momentum, so they need to be shut down. Model active listening and encourage everyone in your group to do the same. This will make your group time a safe space and foster the kind of community that God can use to change people.

The Respond section at the close of the group time is the most dynamic part of this study. During this section, participants are invited to put what they have learned into action. However, for this to be successful, it will require some preparation on your part. So take time to read over this section each week before your group meets, as several of them require special materials. Reading ahead will allow you to ask group members to bring any items you might need but don't have and will give you a sense of how to lead your group through these experiences. Use the supply list below to make sure you have everything you need.

SESSION	LOVE DOES	EVERYBODY, ALWAYS
1	• phones	• Copy of the "YOU" grid for every participant • Pens or pencils
2	• Stick-on nametags (enough for each person to have two) • Pens • A trash can	• One 2" x 4" slip of paper (for every one to write his or her name on) • Additional notebook or sheets of paper for each participant • Pens or pencils • Basket or bowl (for collecting names) • Tape
3	No special materials required outside of the participants' phones. However, you will want to select and screen the YouTube videos ahead of time.	• Index cards (enough for everyone in the group to have one card) • Pens or pencils
4	No special materials required	• Five to six small slips of paper (nothing bigger than 1" x 6") for each participant • Styrofoam coffee cup or Dixie cup (one for each participant) • Pens or pencils
5	• Laptops, tablets, or phones (enough for everyone to do research on the "caper")	• One sheet of paper for each participant • Pens or pencils

Finally, even though there are instructions for how to conclude each session, please feel free to strike out on your own. Just make sure you do something intentional to mark the end of the meeting. It may also be helpful to take time before or after the closing prayer to go over that week's between-session personal study options and ask people what they would like to try. This way, everyone can depart in confidence.

Group Dynamics

Leading a group through *Love Does* and *Everybody, Always* will prove to be highly rewarding both to you and to your group members. However, this doesn't mean you will not encounter any challenges along the way! Discussions can get off track. Group members may not be sensitive to the needs and ideas of others. Some might worry they will be expected to talk about matters that make them feel awkward. Others may express comments that result in disagreements. To help ease this strain on you and the group, consider the following ground rules:

- When someone raises a question or comment that is off the main topic, suggest you deal with it another time, or, if you feel led to go in that direction, let the group know you will be spending some time discussing it.

- If someone asks a question that you don't know how to answer, admit it and move on. At your discretion, feel free to invite the group members to comment on questions that call for personal experience.

- If you find one or two people are dominating the discussion time, direct a few questions to others in the group. Outside the main group time, ask the more dominating members to help you draw out the quieter ones. Work to make them a part of the solution instead of the problem.

- When a disagreement occurs, encourage the group members to process the matter in love. Encourage those on opposite sides to restate what they heard the other side say about the matter, and then invite each side to evaluate if that perception is accurate. Lead the group in examining other scriptures related to the topic and look for common ground.

When any of these issues arise, encourage your members to follow these words from the Bible: "Love one another" (John 13:34); "If it is possible, as far as it depends on you, live at peace with everyone" (Romans 12:18); and "Be quick to listen, slow to speak and slow to become angry" (James 1:19). This will make your group time more rewarding and beneficial for everyone who attends.

Thank you again for your willingness to lead your group! May God reward your efforts and dedication and make your time together in these studies fruitful for him.

Action Guide

Feet . . . *are gross.* This is as true today as it was when Jesus was on the earth some 2,000 years ago. However, in Jesus' day, people's feet were especially gross because they *walked* wherever they went—and there were a lot of animals around. Thus, for sanitary reasons, it became important for hosts to have their guests' feet washed before they entered their homes. This task generally fell to the lowest of the servants, because it was considered the lowest of tasks.

So you can imagine the disciples' surprise one day when Jesus picked up a bucket, wrapped a towel around his waist, and started scrubbing their disgusting feet. Here was their respected teacher performing a humiliating task they considered beneath his status. No wonder Peter protested when it came to be his turn! Yet in performing this simple act of service, Jesus was showing the disciples—and us— how to act toward one another. For Jesus, no act of love for others was too menial or too insignificant.

It's interesting that right after this episode, Jesus told his disciples he was giving them a "new commandment." This commandment was for them to love others *just as he had loved them.* Jesus didn't just discuss what it meant to love at an intellectual level. He put his words into action wherever he went. He healed the sick. He was a friend to the friendless. He encouraged the down-and-out. He refused to let cultural barriers prevent him from reaching those in need. Jesus showed us that God's love is *active.*

This type of love isn't natural for us. It requires a different skill set than we are used to using. And while we *want* to follow Jesus' example, it's often difficult to know where to start. It's easy for us to fall into the trap of thinking we don't have the time, skills, or creative energy to do the task. Or we might wonder if the things we *could* do would really matter in the grand scheme of things. The result? We *don't* act. And by not acting, we miss out on an opportunity.

The goal of this short guide is to give you some practical ideas for demonstrating God's love so this doesn't happen. It is arranged according to five different themes with three activities each that relate to those themes. As you work through this guide, feel free to adapt any of those options in any way you choose to best meet the needs of your group of friends, your group's talents and abilities, and your unique situation.

Remember that God's love is never stationary. It doesn't just keep thinking about what to do or make plans for it. God's love does, and as you do things for others, you will be showing them *you care about them, support them, understand what they are going through, and are willing to get involved in their lives.*

Theme #1: Show Others You Care

In *Love Does*, Bob tells the story of a friend he met in high school named Randy. Randy didn't actually go to high school but worked with an organization called Young Life. Randy tried to talk with Bob about Jesus, but Bob kept him at arm's length. Yet that didn't stop Randy from trying to get to know Bob better.

Bob was not a good student, and eventually he decided to drop out of school and go to Yosemite to climb the massive granite cliffs. When he stopped by Randy's house on his way out of town and told him his plan, his friend asked him to wait a few minutes while he "checked something out." Sometime later, Randy appeared back at the front door with a backpack and a sleeping bag. "Bob," he said, "I'm with you."

Bob tells of how he was taken aback by this request, but he agreed to let Randy come along. When they arrived, Bob applied for a number of different jobs in the Yosemite Valley, but each time he was told there was little work available and no hopes of anything opening up soon. Bob was discouraged, but Randy never said, "I told you so." Instead, he told Bob that he was with him whatever the outcome. Finally, Bob decided to give up and go back home to finish high school.

Once again, Randy said, "Whatever you decide, just know that I'm with you." Bob drove back to Randy's house to drop him off, where he saw Randy's girlfriend's car in the driveway. When he entered the house, he noticed a bunch of opened presents—a stack of plates, some wrapping paper, a coffee maker. Then, from around the corner, Randy's girlfriend appeared and said, "Welcome home, honey." It dawned on Bob that she and Randy had actually just gotten married, and these were wedding presents on the floor.

Randy had chosen to leave with Bob that morning he showed up at his door instead of spending the first few days of his marriage with his new bride. Why? Because Randy loved him and was willing to show it. Randy didn't just say he was there for Bob during this critical point in his life—Randy was *actually, literally* right there with Bob. Randy's actions made a profound impact on Bob's life and changed his view of what it meant to have a relationship with Jesus.

The challenge is for you to show others you care in this way. Instead of just *telling* them that you are concerned about them, the goal is to actually *be present* with them in their lives. The following options will give you some practical ideas for how to do this.

OPTION 1: BRING A MEAL

There's a great story in the Bible where Jesus was teaching huge crowds of people in an isolated place. As the hours passed and evening approached, the disciples knew the people would start getting hungry, and there was nowhere for them to get food. So they asked Jesus to send all the people away. Jesus' answer changed their perspective on caring for others. He told *them* to find something for the people to eat—to bring them a meal! Jesus cared about the people and showed it by being with them and meeting even their most basic needs.

For this option, think of a family who could benefit from receiving a couple of meals that you and/or your group prepare. Perhaps you've heard of a situation in which the mom or dad is suffering with an illness. Or you've learned of someone who is having a crisis with a family member . . . or there is a new baby in the home . . . or the family is experiencing some other type of disruption in the normal flow of life. Instead of just expressing your concern and wishing them the best, take it a step further by bringing them a meal. In this way, you will not only be *doing* something practical for them, but you will be *present* with them during this time of need.

If you are doing this with a group, each member could think of a family and then commit to bringing that family a meal at least once during the upcoming week. Or, during your meeting time, you could brainstorm some names together and determine how to divide up the meal schedule. As you are thinking of names, be sure to consider people not only in your "world" but also at your work, at your gym, in your neighborhood, at your school (if you are a student), or in your children's school (if you are a parent).

Once you have some names in place, determine what days and times you and your group will bring the meals. Remember that while home-cooked meals are great, the goal is to show you care in a practical way—so picking up something ready-made or, if appropriate, giving a gift card to a restaurant nearby can work just as well. Make sure you coordinate who is going to reach out to the people you have selected, and make sure everyone is clear as to the dates and times when they are scheduled to bring the meal. Finally, use this as an opportunity to check in with the person or family to see how they are doing. Offer to pray for them (and actually do so), be there to listen, and give them space and quiet as needed to share. Give updates to your group and determine if any adjustments need to be made to the plan. As you do, you will be demonstrating you care.

Option 2: Be a Mentor

In the opening story, you saw how Randy served as a mentor for Bob. Randy didn't instruct Bob by *telling* him the mistakes he was making or by pointing out the right choices he should be making. Instead, Randy chose to be with Bob to experience life with him on his ill-fated trip to Yosemite . . . and to be there when Bob came to the realization that things weren't working out.

For this option, consider a person you know who could benefit from having you as this type of mentor. Maybe there is a young person in your church who seems lonely or has some difficult decisions to make in the days ahead. Perhaps you know of someone who has made some mistakes and is dealing with the hard consequences of those decisions. Or maybe there is an individual who has experienced loss and would just enjoy spending time with you.

Once you have a person in mind, reach out to him or her and set up a time to meet. You can pick a simple activity that the person enjoys—bowling at the local alley, playing basketball at a nearby court, jogging around the neighborhood, taking a walk in a park, shopping at a favorite store. Or, if the person likes projects, you could teach them a skill you know—fixing a car, sewing a piece of clothing, building a piece of furniture.

Whatever you choose, remember that the point is to be with them, to listen to them, and to not judge them. Offer advice if it is requested, but don't fall into the trap of viewing them as a "project." As you do, you will be showing that person you care about him or her—and in this way you might just give them a glimpse of the love God has for them.

Option 3: Reach Out to Prisoners

When you read the Bible, you find stories of a lot of different people who, for one reason or another, ended up in prison. A guy named Joseph was falsely accused of making moves on his master's wife and ended up in prison. Peter, the disciple, spent time in prison before an angel broke him out—much to the surprise of Peter's friends. Paul, who wrote most of the New Testament, was thrown into prison on many occasions.

Jesus even told a story where he commended those who gave the hungry something to eat, the thirsty something to drink, the stranger a place to stay, and the *prisoners* a friend to visit them and care for them in their time of need. Those same types of needs are still present in our world today—especially in the families of those who have a member in prison. Unfortunately, these needs are typically overlooked, even by those in the church.

For this option, consider some things you can do to help the families of prisoners and show them that God hasn't forgotten them. Perhaps the family needs help with yard work, or some things fixed around the house, or could benefit from some other act of service. Perhaps the husband or wife of the incarcerated member would just like someone to talk with who wouldn't judge his or her family. You could be a listening ear to them and, in the process, show them that God hasn't shunned them either.

Another option is to work with an organization such as Prison Fellowship, which excels at ministering to prisoners and their families (see prisonfellowship.org). On this website, you can read about the needs of prisoners and their families, how Prison Fellowship seeks to help them through programs such as Angel Tree (which focuses on helping children who have parents in prison), and how you can help by either donating funds or volunteering. The Prison Fellowship website also contains resources to help you aid the family in coping with their loss, support their loved ones behind bars, and prepare for reentry into society.

Whatever option you choose, make sure you keep the focus on helping the family know that *you are with them* and support them. As you do, you will be showing them that *love does*.

Theme #2: Show Support to Others

When Bob was a kid, he had a great relationship with his dad. His father had a rifle that he used on hunting trips, and on occasion he would let Bob hold it. Bob would listen as his father taught him how to have a healthy respect for the gun, how to look through the scope, and how to be careful and precise as he pulled the trigger.

Bob would like to pretend he was on the trail of a grizzly bear when he was allowed to hold the gun. One day, Bob asked his father if he could "hunt the grizzly." His dad considered the request, and then checked the chamber of the rifle to make sure it didn't contain a round. Bob lifted the gun to his eye, aimed at a pretend target, took a breath, and pulled the trigger. As it turns out, there was a bullet in the gun.

The bullet tore through the wall, and Bob took the full recoil from the gun on his right eye. When he came to, he saw that his T-shirt was drenched in blood. Bob's first thought was that he was in trouble and would get spanked. But as he looked through his bloody eye, he only saw concern on his father's face. His dad scooped him up and took him to the hospital, where the doctors stitched him up.

We often get the idea that we're always falling short and that God is mad at us for the things we've done. We've tried to hit the right target and do good, but somehow things went wrong and we ended up on our backs in a blood-soaked T-shirt. At such times, God isn't standing over us and enjoying the pain we've inflicted on ourselves. He is more like Bob's dad, who scooped him up into his arms and carried him away to get healed.

The way we view God's love for us will determine how we share that love with others. If we view God as judgmental and eager to punish, we will treat others that way as well. But if we view God as a caring father—like the Bible says he is—then we will come to their aid when they miss the mark. That is the goal of this challenge: to support others and pick them up when they are down, just as God picks us up when we are down.

OPTION 1: ENCOURAGE SOMEONE

In the Bible, we see that Paul knew about this type of love from God firsthand. When we first read about him, he was putting followers of Christ to death. But an encounter with Jesus on the road to Damascus changed everything. Paul experienced God's grace in a profound way, and he went from being a Christian-killer to a church planter.

Over the course of his life, Paul would be beaten, pelted with stones, imprisoned, shipwrecked, and basically live in constant danger from those who wanted to stop him from talking about Jesus. But Paul never gave up. Not only that, but he also never gave up encouraging others who were also experiencing difficulties. Today, we have two of Paul's letters to his close friend Timothy, and one to his friend Titus, to encourage them to never give up sharing about God—even in the face of trials.

Can you remember a time when you received a word of encouragement from someone like this? If you can, how did it make you feel? Did it turn a bad day into a good one? This challenge is to think of someone who needs your support and to reach out to that person with some encouragement. This could be a family member, a co-worker, a neighbor, or a friend you haven't seen in a while. Note that you don't need to write a letter as long as Paul's to his friends in order to brighten their day. Just a few simple words can go a long way to brighten someone's day, show them you are with them, and motivate them to keep going forward.

In Paul's day, letters had to be dictated and hand-carried to faraway places. But today you have many means of sending a note to someone—via email, text messages, social media, and the like (though the personal handwritten note is still a nice touch). So take advantage of all these means and tell someone you support them and know what they are going through. You might never know the impact you will have on someone when you do.

Option 2: Support Someone in Need

Who is someone in your world who needs to be picked up off the ground? Perhaps not in the literal sense—like Bob needed to be picked up by his dad—but someone who has hit a rough patch lately and could use some help. What could you do to show support to that person? Or maybe you don't know the individual personally. Maybe it's a homeless person you see each day on your way to work. What could you do to show that God cares?

In the Bible, we find story after story of Jesus helping people who are in need. Some of these people he knew, like his friend Peter's mother-in-law. Most of these people he did not know, like the crowds who flocked to him to hear his teaching. In each case, we see that Jesus figured out what people really needed and steered them toward that. He healed the sick and hurting, and he spent time with those who were looked at as "less than" in society.

This option is to simply support someone in need. You could do this by spending some time with the person, doing something he or she likes doing, and then using the time to encourage that individual. Maybe you have a friend who enjoys cooking. Make a meal together as you talk. Perhaps you know a young person who likes sports. Shoot some hoops together as you talk. Or maybe you know an outdoorsy person who would like to share with you as you hike or take a walk together.

And don't forget the needs of those whom you might not know. Consider volunteering at a local kitchen or homeless shelter. Or visit a nursing home or hospital and be a friend to someone who is lonely. You could even find a person in need as close as your neighbor, who could use your help while he or she is recovering from a sickness or unable to do more physical chores. Just be creative! As you do, you will be showing others that God supports them.

Option 3: Share Your Story

If you've spent any time with Christians or in the church, you have no doubt heard them talk about their *testimony*. The word might bring to mind a picture of a person on the witness stand in court, but actually all it refers to is that person's *story* of how he or she found Jesus. In Bob's case, he came to know about Christ through a high school friend. This friend, named Doug, believed in Jesus, but he wasn't a wimp. He was fun-loving, adventurous, and a bit mischievous.

Bob liked the fact that Doug could be friends with Jesus and still shoot pellet guns. He liked that Doug wasn't one of those "perfect" people that you seem to see on Sundays at church. Doug was real, and that made Jesus real to Bob as well. Because of Doug's influence, Bob came to believe in Christ. The same can be true of you. Your story can be a powerful tool to help you relate to others, show support, and tell them that God cares about them.

So this option is to look for ways to support others by sharing your story. Now, this doesn't mean that you have to sit the person down and tell him or her in detail how you came to Christ (though you could). You could just share an experience that would help the person with something he or she is facing in the present moment. Maybe you have gone through a similar situation that the person is facing and could offer some perspective on the problem.

As Bob writes in *Love Does*, it was more about what he *saw* in Doug than what Doug had to say to him. So don't forget the *testimony* of your life. If you actively love others, people will notice, and they will wonder what is different about you. They may not be attracted to *religion*, but they will be attracted to what they see in you. Your story may not only support them but also lead them to understand that God is real and cares for them where they are.

Theme #3: Show Audacious Love for Others

When you are young and in love, you will stop at nothing to show your affections to that one special person. As Bob writes in *Love Does*, he came across one such lovestruck young man named Ryan who was walking on a path near his house. Right off the bat, Ryan told Bob how he was passionately in love with his girlfriend. He then asked if he could use Bob's house to propose to her. Bob was taken aback by Ryan's forwardness, but he agreed.

But Ryan's requests did not stop there. A few days later, Bob saw Ryan again skipping up the path. He stopped at Bob's house again and, after some pauses, asked if it would be okay for him to have dinner in Bob's backyard the night of the proposal. Bob was impressed with the depth of Ryan's love for his girlfriend and agreed. He looked forward to seeing how far Ryan would go to set up the perfect evening to show his love for this girl.

Next, Ryan asked if he could have his friends over to serve dinner. And not just a handful of people—but twenty friends in Bob's house. A few days later, the question was whether they could put speakers in Bob's backyard so they could dance after dinner. Finally, Ryan came bounding up with one final request: Could he use Bob's boat after dinner and dancing? Ryan's requests were outrageous—even ridiculous. But Bob agreed to everything, and he even put his own touch on the evening by getting the Coast Guard to put on a display of their own.

Ryan's audacious love was on full display the night of the proposal. It reminded Bob of those parts in the Bible where Jesus talks about his audacious love for his "bride." The kind of love that Jesus talked about is one that never grows tired, or stale, or expected. It is a type of love that never finishes finding ways to fully express itself.

This challenge is to find ways that you and your group can show audacious love to others. While the options you choose might not be as bold and over-the-top as Ryan's requests, the goal is to get out of your comfort zone a bit and take some risks for others. As you do, you will be showing the world that God is real, powerful, and at work in their lives.

OPTION 1: USE YOUR PASSION

You can't deny that Ryan had *passion*—not only for his bride-to-be but also to make the night of his proposal something she would never forget. Ryan used his passion, and his skills at planning, to create the perfect evening (with Bob's help). Ryan's passion motivated him to make outlandish requests, dream big, and see the plan through to completion.

How often do you exhibit this same type of passion when it comes to loving others? How are you using your particular interests to help another person? Is there something you could be doing more to show someone that God deeply cares about him or her?

The goal of this option is for you and your group to take an inventory of your skills, identify what motivates you, and look for ways to put your passions to work. You can do this by actually brainstorming and making a list, or you could just consider what it is you most like to do during your free time. Do you like working on cars? If so, offer to help someone in your community with their car repairs. Are you good with fixing broken things? Then offer to help a neighbor fix something in his or her house. Do you enjoy sewing? Offer to mend or even make something for a person whom you know is in financial need.

If your passion is for *leading*, you could volunteer to be a co-leader of a youth group or a Girl Scout troop. Maybe you are great at sports, and helping coach a youth community team would be a great use of your time. You might be a veteran shopper who could go to the store for someone who can't easily get out of the house. Consider partnering with a friend or family member to see how your skills could play off each other to make an even greater impact.

You may not think your skills and passions could be of any use to others. But don't underestimate them! No matter what your passion is—or how insignificant you might think it is—God can use it to show his audacious love.

Option 2: Commit Random Acts of Kindness

Have you ever been on the receiving end of a random act of kindness? If so, you know what a great feeling it brings. It's nice to know that someone is thinking of you and wants to do something to lift you up. It's encouraging to realize the person thinks so highly of you that he or she is willing to go out of his or her way on your behalf.

Jesus was amazing at committing random acts of kindness. In the Bible, we read that he traveled from place to place to show God's audacious love in practical ways. He broke social barriers by inviting a despised tax collector to have dinner with him. He spoke with lepers and actually touched them as well. He told the disciples to let children come to him. Time and again he sought the down-and-outers and lifted them up.

Your goal in this option is to demonstrate random acts of kindness to another person. Perhaps, as in Bob's case, this could be saying *yes* to an outlandish request from someone—a request you would normally answer with a *no*. Or it could be offering to watch a friend's kids so he and his wife can have dinner together. Or you could offer to pay for the car behind you in the drive-thru at Starbucks or McDonald's. Or you could look for someone who needs help at the grocery store and offer to load the bags into his or her car.

Showing God's acts of kindness to others doesn't have to be a well-orchestrated event like Ryan planned for his future bride. It can be a random act. The point is just to do something out of the ordinary that will lift up a person's spirit and put a smile on his or her face. So take some time to think about how you could do a little something "extra" for someone.

Option 3: Be a Co-conspirator with God

Ryan was clearly a young man "out of control" and had no idea how big a request he was making when he asked Bob to borrow his boat. After all, Bob was someone he had just met! But as Bob notes, "To Ryan, I wasn't a total stranger—no one was. To him, the whole world was full of co-conspirators when it came to winning over his love."

Do you see yourself as a co-conspirator with God when it comes to winning people over with his love? If so, what are some things you and your group of friends will "conspire" to do with him? If not, what is getting in the way of you seeing others this way?

This option is all about looking for ways that you and your group can join forces with others to serve the needs in your community. Perhaps you could join with a local shelter to offer clothing or other personal items to those in need. You and your group could collect these items during the week and then deliver them in person on the weekend. Or you could choose to offer a financial gift to support a charity in your region. You could even purchase some gift cards at a fast-food restaurant or grocery store and give them out to those who need them.

This doesn't have to be complex. Sometimes, the best thing you can do for someone is to just offer an understanding ear. All too often, people in need are given pat answers and clichés, when what they really need is to be heard. You could conspire with God this week to make a difference in that person's life simply by being present and willing to listen.

Theme #4: Serve Others Selflessly

Back in 2004, the Walt Disney Company released a computer-animated superhero film called *The Incredibles*. The movie was different from the standard run-of-the-mill superhero films in that it focused on a family who had special powers—and who were trying to lead a normal suburban life. As the movie opens, the father is working as a claims adjuster for an insurance company, but he knows that's not the real him. So, when he loses his temper with his boss and is subsequently fired, he seizes the opportunity to become "Mr. Incredible" again and starts to do some covert superhero work for a mysterious woman named Mirage.

The father is re-energized by the work, but he quickly discovers that he needs a new superhero outfit. So he creates some drawings and takes them to a friend named Edna, who makes costumes. However, each time he shows his ideas, Edna tells him to *lose the cape*. When he asks why, Edna shows him examples of different superheroes who ran into all kinds of problems when they wore capes. Thunderhead's cape snagged on a missile. Stratogale's cape caught in a jet engine. Splashdown's cape was sucked into a tornado. "No capes!" she says.

Edna's point, as Bob likewise explains in *Love Does*, is that you can just get a lot more stuff done without a cape. Jesus would agree. In the Bible, when we see him doing something amazing—something *incredible*—he often instructs those who witnessed the miracle to "tell no one." Jesus was saying that when we do something for others, we need to lose the flashy cape of self-promotion. We need to be secretly incredible for God.

Secretly incredible people go on capers without the cape. They give away their time and resources without seeking credit for their trouble. They commit to praying for others who are in need without asking what is in it for themselves. So the goal is for you and your group to join this elite bunch of capeless wonders—to go above the norm in how you show your concern.

OPTION 1: SERVE SELFLESSLY IN YOUR COMMUNITY

There are numerous examples in the Bible of Jesus serving others in secret. When he raised a little girl from the dead, he said, "Tell no one." When he met a man with leprosy and healed him, he said, "Tell no one." When he healed two guys who were blind, he said to one of them, "Say nothing to anyone." Jesus modeled *humility* for us in serving.

For this option, your goal is to love and serve others without them knowing you are loving and serving them. Begin by brainstorming some ways that you and your group can be awesome without promoting your awesomeness. (This means no social media posts or tweets!) Maybe you would like to mow a friend's yard or pull some weeds in the flower beds when he or she is out for a while. Perhaps you could covertly wash a friend's car or clean the gutters on his or her house. You could even drop an anonymous note in that person's mailbox to encourage him or her and let that person know people are praying for him or her.

And don't forget about the people you *don't* know. If you see a need, find a way to meet it without donning a cape. Buy some groceries or clothes for a family you know is in need and drop it off at their front door. Purchase some gift cards and mail them to someone without including your name on the return address. Contribute cans of food to a local food bank or money to a charity that supports the poor in your community.

After doing this act of service, reflect on what it was like to give to others in this way. How did the experience change you? How did it make you feel? What was easy or difficult? Compare notes with friends or members of your group who also served in this manner.

OPTION 2: SERVE SELFLESSLY AT YOUR "CHURCH"

In the Bible, we hear a lot about guys like Peter, James, John, and Paul, and all they did for the first community of Jesus-followers. We hear less about guys like Matthias, who was chosen to replace Judas as a disciple, and even less about Justus, who lost out on the job to Matthias. In fact, we never hear about Justus again after his brief mention in the Bible.

This doesn't mean, however, that Justus was less significant just because he didn't get the same amount of attention as the others. Justus certainly went on sharing about God and what it meant to follow Jesus. He went on serving in the early church. In the same way, we need to be people who will go on serving and meeting needs in our world even if we don't get any notoriety for our acts.

For this option, think of specific things you can do to help others in your church. This could involve volunteering to vacuum or clean up the youth room before the next service. Or it could be volunteering to fill in for someone at the front counter on Sunday to give that person a break. Maybe you could just tell your pastor that you and your group would like to man the coffee counter, or serve as ushers, or greet people that week at the door.

Remember that the church doesn't necessarily involve a building. As Bob notes in *Love Does*, the church is "a vibrant community of people consisting of two or more of varied backgrounds gathering around Jesus." Wherever you find yourself surrounded by people who meet this definition, look for ways that you can serve them. Simply ask, "How are you doing? What problems are you facing? What can I do to help you this week?"

After you have done this, reflect on what it was like to serve in this way. What did you enjoy about volunteering? What needs did you uncover as you did this? What does this motivate you to do in the future when it comes to helping your fellow Jesus-followers? Compare notes with friends or members of your group who also served in this manner.

Option 3: Serve Selflessly in Prayer

Studies have shown that about half of Americans say they pray every day. Women on average pray a bit more regularly than men, and Americans aged sixty-five or older pray more frequently than their under-thirty counterparts. But what's most interesting in these studies is what Americans pray *for*. Most people pray for families or friends, followed by their own problems, and then about good things that happened to them.

In this option, your challenge is to go against this trend. Each day this week, focus on praying for the needs of others rather than yourself. You may want to do this by creating a prayer journal where you write down the names of people you know and the issues they are facing. From there, expand your list to pray for the needs of people you don't know, such as people affected by a natural disaster, a community that is in need, a person or family you hear about in the news, or even your leaders in government.

Consider joining with a friend or a group of friends at some point during the week to share your lists and pray together. Then, when the week is over, go back and consider what it was like to pray in this way. What did you learn about yourself from the experience? In what ways, if any, will this change the way you pray in the future? What does it mean for you to "lose the cape" when it comes to showing God's love to others? Be sure to compare notes with friends or the members of your group to get their perspectives as well.

Theme #5: Take Risks for Others

The word *risk* brings different images to mind. For some, risk means moving a degree outside of their comfort zone, like ordering a new item at their favorite restaurant, or talking to someone across the room, or changing up their routine a bit. For others, risk means something a bit more extreme, like parachuting out of a plane, or climbing a rock wall, or bungee jumping off of a high bridge.

Bob's friend Don Valencia was a guy who took these kinds of risks. He loved to backpack and race cars and climb mountains. He would tell Bob stories of sleeping high above the tree line in the wild or racing his car for twenty-four hours just to see if he could do it. Don was an amazing person who seemed to live on the edge of death.

This adventurous side made him shine in his career as a cell biologist. Don actually played with some of the world's deadliest diseases by freeze-drying cells so he could study them. He even tried this freeze-drying technique on some coffee beans his wife bought to see if he could brew a good cup of coffee out in the wild. To his surprise, the coffee was amazing. Later, he shared his experiment with the CEO of Starbucks, and it wasn't long before Don was working in a multimillion-dollar laboratory for the company. Don went on to invent a carbonated cold coffee that failed completely—but this concoction eventually led to the Frappuccino, one of the most popular drinks at the coffee chain.

After retiring from Starbucks, Don used his risk-taking skills to serve the rural poor in Central America, Mexico, and other places around the world. He even moved his family to Central America so they could immerse themselves in the culture. Don found himself closer to God in the incredible adventure of helping those in need.

The theme of this challenge is for you to think about what *risk* means to you and how you can push yourself to serve others. While your definition of *risk* might not involve traveling to faraway places or immersing yourself in a different culture, there is always something you can do to show risky love to others.

OPTION 1: REACH OUT TO A STRANGER

There's a great story Jesus told in the Bible about a man who was going on a journey from one city to another. Unfortunately, the region in which the man was traveling was full of bandits, and a group of them attacked the man and left him for dead. Two men from his own culture happened upon him in the road, but they passed him by.

Then a man whom he would normally consider his enemy came by. The injured man must have thought this person would pass him by as well, but instead he helped the man onto his donkey, bandaged his wounds, and even helped him get to the next town. There he paid for the injured man's stay so he would get the best care. This stranger took risks for the injured man and was, as Jesus stated, a good neighbor to him. We would call him a Good Samaritan.

For this option, take a risk and reach out to a stranger in need. Perhaps, like the man in Jesus' story, this actually involves helping someone in need of medical attention or shelter. Maybe it involves buying a meal for a person who has obviously gone for some time without food. But it could also mean talking to a new person in a group you belong to, just to make him or her feel welcome . . . or it could mean reaching out to people in your neighborhood who have different beliefs and finding some common ground.

The important thing is to keep your eyes open and look for ways you can be a good neighbor to someone you don't know. As you do, you will show that person that God sees past the boundaries people so often set up between themselves. You will not only make an impact on that person's life but will also demonstrate God's love is at work in this world.

OPTION 2: BE A PARTNER IN ADVENTURE

When you are following after God, you take risks like Don Valencia. You have a confidence that God is leading your way and you have nothing to fear. While you know you will encounter setbacks, hardships, and obstacles, you can rest in the fact that God is with you in the journey. Even more, you can partner with others in their journey and help them along.

The challenge in this option is to consider areas where you can get involved on a longer-term basis. For instance, you might partner with an organization that is seeking to meet the needs of those in lesser-developed countries. One such organization is Love Does (lovedoes.org), which fights for freedom and human rights, works to improve educational opportunities, and assists those in need of a voice and a friend. YWAM (Youth With A Mission) Latvia has an outreach called Freedom 61 (riga.ywamlatvia.org) focused on those caught in human trafficking in that country.

If you feel more compelled to meet the needs of your community, consider volunteering at organizations that minister to the homeless, single parents, kids in foster care, the elderly, or people battling addictions. Or volunteer at pregnancy centers, or work with charities that conduct clothing drives, or partner with others in fundraising. You could even go on a short-term missions trip or sign up with Habitat for Humanity to build homes for families who could not otherwise afford to have a roof over their heads (see habitat.org).

Whatever you choose, be willing to take some risks and be stretched a bit in the process. Commit to doing the project for a set amount of time and then reflect on the experience and see where it leads you next. After all, you never know where you will end up when you start taking risks and showing people that God cares for them.

OPTION 3: DREAM BIG!

Big dreams can lead to big results. As Bob relates in *Love Does*, after the events of September 11, 2001, he asked his kids, "If you had five minutes in front of a group of world leaders, what would you ask them to help make sense of life, faith, hope, and the events that are unfolding around them?" Bob had them write down what they would ask on a piece of paper.

Adam, the youngest, asked if the leaders would like to come over to his house. Richard asked what each of the world leaders was hoping for. Lindsey, the oldest, asked if she and her brothers could visit *them*. Bob put all the ideas into a letter and helped them find the addresses of every world leader through the CIA website. Then they mailed the letters. Hundreds of them.

Of course, the responses that came back said, "Thanks, but no thanks." All but one—from the State House in Bulgaria, which offered them an invitation to the palace. Then another invitation arrived from the prime minister of Switzerland. And then one from the president of Israel. In the end, the kids received *twenty-nine* invitations.

Love Does when you take risks and dream big. So, this challenge is for you to think about everything you have learned in *Love Does* and *Everybody, Always* and just run with it. What are some dreams that go beyond the length of this campaign? How can you make those dreams a reality? Who do you need to partner with to help you? What goals do you need to set?

If you have been putting *this* into action with a group, you can start by getting ideas from each person. List the steps you would need to accomplish to launch your adventure along with how you will chart your progress. Consider what resources you will need—and then pray boldly that God will provide for those needs and guide your efforts. Finally, expect the unexpected and celebrate when you see God making your big dreams a reality!

About Bob Goff

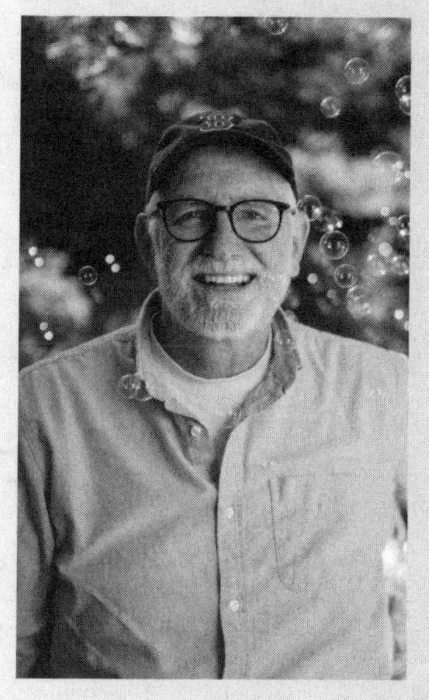

Bob Goff is the *New York Times* bestselling author of *Love Does*; *Everybody, Always*; *Live in Grace, Walk in Love*; *Dream Big*; *Undistracted*; *Catching Whimsy*; and *Love Does for Kids*. He's a lover of balloons, cake pops, and helping people pursue their big dreams. Bob's greatest ambitions in life are to love others, do stuff, and most importantly, to hold hands with his wife, Sweet Maria, and spend time with their amazing family. For more, check out BobGoff.com and LoveDoes.org.

Connect with Bob

Bob's passion is people. He'd love to hear from you if you want to email him at info@bobgoff.com. You can also follow him on Instagram and X: @bobgoff. Here's his cell phone number if you want to give him a call: (619) 985-4747.

Bob is available to inspire and engage your team, organization, or audience. To date, he's spoken to more than two million people, bringing his unique perspective and exciting storytelling with him. He is a personal coach and hosts various workshops at The Oaks, a retreat center in Southern California.

To learn more about coaching, Bob's workshops, or to inquire about speaking opportunities, check out bobgoff.com.